THE
MEN WHO
STARE AT
HENS

THE MEN WHO STARE AT HENS

Great Irish Eccentrics
from W.B. Yeats to Brendan Behan

SIMON LEYLAND

The History Press Ireland

For my Mother and Father
Non procul a proprio stipite poma cadunt

First published 2019

The History Press
The Mill, Brimscome Port
Stroud, Gloucestershire
GL5 2QG

www.thehistorypress.ie

British Library Cataloguing in Publication Data.
A catalogue record for this book is available from the British Library.

ISBN 978 0 7509 8927 5

Typesetting and origination by The History Press
Printed in Great Britain by TJ International Ltd, Padstow, Cornwall

ACKNOWLEDGEMENTS

My thanks go to the wonderful Ronan Colgan of The History Press Ireland for his exceptionally good taste in deciding to publish this book.

A doff of the hat goes to Lauren Newby, Project Editor, and a firm hand shake to Katie Beard, Designer, for her delightful book cover.

I would also like to acknowledge the Letterfrack Council of Elders, who individually and collectively gave me the idea of writing a book on eccentrics, and the management and staff of the Veldons Seafarer Bar for allowing me to use their premises as an office.

Finally, my enduring thanks to the fragrant one for typing out endless drafts and being nice to me.

ABOUT THE AUTHOR

Simon Leyland has been living in Connemara since 2008. In a previous life he was a City trader and as a result has always been interested in the strange and absurd.

He has had three volumes of poetry published: *Ramblings of an Unkempt Man* (Erbacce Press, 2010), *The Language of Exile* (Erbacce Press, 2011) and *Codes for Living Quietly* (Erbacce Press, 2012). He has also written *A Curious Guide to London* (Bantam Press, 2014) and was shortlisted for the Hennessey Prize.

When behind on the rent he writes articles about cricket and horse racing for various magazines.

A blog exists at simonleyland.net.

INTRODUCTION

John Stuart Mill once said that 'Eccentricity has always abounded when and where strength of character has abounded. And the amount of eccentricity in a society has been proportional to the amount of genius, mental vigour and moral courage it contained.'

Wise words, for we all have our own queer little quirks, odd habits and weird idiosyncrasies. Eccentricity is perhaps merely the amplification of this behaviour and madness is a leap in the dark. It is no crime to be an individual – especially in these times of suffocating bureaucracy, where people are reduced to just numbers or, worse still, ciphers.

Eccentrics, at least for my purposes, are also funny. They deviate from the norm in ways so odd and quirky that one wonders what made them think of it, not to mention what drove them to act out their ideas.

Quite recently there has been some serious research into eccentricity. According to the psychologist David Weeks, it appears that eccentrics are more cheerful than normal people. He goes on to contend that it is easy to distinguish between eccentrics and the mentally ill: the eccentrics are happy.

Like everything else, eccentricity has fashions and behaviour that go unnoticed in one age, but seem bizarre in another. The eccentricities of the Cork-born vegetarian 'Linen' Cook may have seemed outrageous in his time, but today he would have been viewed as a relatively normal, Guardian-reading, card-carrying Greenpeace activist.

You will no doubt notice that some of the entrants in this homage to eccentricity are not, strictly speaking, Irish. I therefore refer you to the late, great Conor Cruise O'Brien who said that 'Irishness is not primarily a question of birth or blood or language; it is the condition of being involved in the Irish situation, and usually of being mauled by it.'

This book is a panegyric to all the strange scientists, magnificent misers, unhinged politicians, ritual compulsives, barmy builders, bizarre adventurers, brilliant iconoclasts, crackpot visionaries and the touchingly deluded.

I therefore propose to make 1 April, National Eccentrics Day. When the day arrives, do something different: wear your clothes back to front, invent something that no one will want, pay your mortgage with vegetables, or go to work in a wheelbarrow pulled by sheep. Perhaps you already do. Congratulations. We really do *need* our eccentrics.

RICHARD WHATLEY (1787-1863)

One of the strangest clerics Dublin had ever seen was the wonderfully hyperactive Archbishop of Dublin, Richard Whatley.

A man of many odd interests, including boomerang-throwing and climbing trees, he believed that an outdoor life was the cure for all ills. If he ever had a headache, he would go out in his shirtsleeves, whatever the weather, and chop down a tree; the problem was that it could be any tree that took his fancy.He also objected to wasting money, but his congregation felt that he was taking it too far when he started to use worn-out church vestments for gardening.

His inability to sit still struck terror into the hearts of hostesses, as anyone who invited Whatley into their homes could expect to be left with broken tables and chairs. This was due to his uncontrollable habit of twitching, rocking violently and kicking out at anything in range whilst sitting down. His record seems to have been six chairs during an evening with Lord Burghley, who then had a chair specially built for Whatley's next visit with legs 'like the balustrade of Dublin castle'. Lady Anglesey, however, banned him from ever visiting again after he broke her best china when he managed to kick over a cabinet.

One day the Chief Justice was sitting next to Whatley at a Privy Council meeting and, feeling a sneeze coming on, put his hand in his pocket for his handkerchief – only to find the Archbishop's foot already there. Large crowds would turn up for Whatley's sermons, not to hear him preach but to see what he would do. One member of his congregation recorded that he 'worked his leg about to such an extent that it glided over the edge of the pulpit and hung there until he had finished'. He would give lectures to his students while lying flat on a sofa with his legs dangling over the arm. Sometimes they were invited to accompany him on walks, which usually involved climbing trees.

He was totally disinterested in social chit-chat: whilst dining in company, he would take out a pair of scissors and trim his nails, or make miniature boomerangs out of his visiting cards and send them flying around the room.

Another example of his peculiar outlook on life was when a notoriously lazy clergyman asked Whatley for permission to go to New Zealand for his health. He replied, 'By all means go to New Zealand – you are so lean that no Maori could eat you without loathing.'

He was also keen on phrenology, the once fashionable science of determining a person's character traits by the size and shape of their head. He created a phrenological test of his own, namely: 'Take a handful of peas and drop them on the head of a patient, the amount of the man's dishonesty will depend on the number which remain there. If a large number remain, kindly tell your butler to lock up the silver.'

BASIL MACLEAR (1881-1915)

Sport and fashion have always been strange bedfellows. The sight of David Beckham cavorting around in a sarong is still enough to put you off your breakfast, and now it appears that even Conor McGregor is getting on in the act with his ridiculous suits.

There was one man, however, who managed to carry it off with great aplomb. He was a rugby player called Basil

Maclear and he played eleven times for Ireland between 1905 and 1907. Having a reputation as a man about town, he was also well known for his sharp dress sense, which he brought with him onto the rugby pitch. Maclear would start the game with a pair of beautifully cut white calfskin gloves which he would then replace with another pair at half time. He surpassed himself during a match against Wales when he scored two tries wearing his customary white calfskin gloves plus a pair of 'blancoed' military putees.

The South African rugby historian AC Parker described Maclear's try aginst South Africa in 1905 as 'one of the greatest individual efforts ever achieved at international level'.

Sadly our elegant friend died of his wounds in 1915 after the Battle of Ypres.

BEAUCHAMP BAGENAL (1741-1802)

Beauchamp Bagenal's behaviour on the Grand Tour both appalled and astonished his contemporaries. Jonah Barrington, the lawyer, politician and memoirist of Abbeyleix, included an account of the adventures of Beauchamp Bagenal in his memoirs. He wrote that Bagenal 'fought a prince, jilted a princess, intoxicated the Doge of Venice, carried off a duchess from Madrid, scaled the walls of a convent in Lisbon and fought a duel in Paris'.

The jilted princess, Princess Charlotte of Mecklenburgh-Strelitz, you will no doubt be relieved to hear, consoled herself by marrying George III.

At home in Dunleckney, County Carlow, 'King' Bagenal (as he was known) entertained a never-ending procession of guests and spongers on a grand scale. They repaid him by obedience to his whims, not always a simple task.

Meals at Dunleckney were meals in name only; they were first and foremost drinking contests. Sitting in his favourite chair at the head of the table, Bagenal kept a couple of fully loaded pistols by his side. One was used to shoot the top off the cask(s) of claret that were inevitably drunk at each sitting, and the other, combined with a baleful glare, was a not so gentle reminder that all glasses must be emptied. If that was not bad enough, worse was to follow. He would then insist on his guests performing feats of strength and making them wrestle against each other, whilst more claret flowed.

One poor guest, a clergyman, who quickly realised that he would not be able to keep up, actually ran off and climbed up a tree rather than be obliged to take part. He later described the scene the next morning, when 'such of the company as were still able to walk' piled the bodies of their insensible companions onto a cart and delivered them to their respective homes.

In an age of obsessive duelling, Beauchamp Bagenall adored the prospect of a good fight. As a Mr Neill O'Daunt put it, 'he had a tender affection for pistols. He was eager to pass his wisdom on to the younger generation, and derived great delight from encouraging the young men who frequented his house to hunt, drink, and solve points of honour at twelve paces.'

He even provoked his godson, Beauchamp Bagenal Harvey, to a duel. Harvey shot first and missed, whereupon Bagenal, immensely pleased, exclaimed, 'Damn you, you young rascal! Do you know that you had like to kill your godfather? Go back to Dunleckney, you dog, and have a good breakfast got ready for us. I only wanted to see if you were stout.'

When Bagenal became lame due to an unwanted souvenir from an old skirmish, he preferred to lean against a tombstone when fighting a duel. However for his very last duel, he decided to rewrite the rules: he would fight it from his chair. This came about after a neighbour's pig had strayed on to his land and the obviously delighted Bagenal, now with cause to pick an argument, sent a provocative letter to his neighbour to demand satisfaction. Bagenal was well into his sixties by this time and gout ridden. On the day of the duel, a chair was carried out to the site of the duel and Bagenal sat and waited. On the appointed hour, after they both exchanged shots, the neighbour was severely wounded. Apart from the arm of his chair being blown off, the mighty Bagenal was unharmed.

He appears to have died from a fit on the evening of 1 May 1802 after drinking three bottles of claret and a bottle of port with his dinner.

W.B. YEATS (1825-1939)

William Butler Yeats was fascinated by the occult and was a member of a rather odd sect known as the Hermetic Order of the Golden Dawn. A fervent believer in ghosts, he joined something called 'The Ghost Club' as well.

An astrological chart drawn up through the Golden Dawn told Yeats that October 1917 was the most auspicious time to get married and get married he did, to the 25-year-old Georgie Hyde-Lees in October 1917. Shortly afterwards he developed a habit of writing while in a trance like state, which he called 'spirit writing'. It appeared to work best when he was moving, so any time he was on a bus or a train he would go into a 'compositional trance', which involved staring straight ahead, humming to himself and beating time with his hands to the sound of wheels going round. People would often come up to him and ask him if he was all right.

He could not spell, but in this he was in good company as Hemingway, Einstein, Keats and Churchill were also notoriously bad spellers. But he had to wait until he was in his fifties before he was recognised as a truly great poet, and this caused him some anxiety, as he now found himself surrounded by adoring young women. The resulting distractions caused him to suffer from both impotence and writer's block.

His creative muse having fled and being unable to 'get it up', he took matters into his own hands (figuratively speaking) by experimenting with various cures to achieve what was known in polite society of the time as 'rejuvenation'. In 1934 he went to a (subsequently discredited) Viennese doctor called Eugene Steinach for a type of vasectomy, a procedure known as 'Steinaching'. Just to be on the safe side he also injected himself with monkey glands. It obviously did the trick, as a few months later he was escorting a beautiful young actress, Margot Ruddock, forty years his junior, after which the Irish press called him 'The Gland Old Man of Letters'.

Yeats called these years his second puberty, and when he was not chasing young women or writing poetry he was also in the habit of hypnotising hens.

MARY MONCKTON (1746-1840)

Described as 'very short, very fat but handsome, splendidly and fantastically dressed', Mary Monckton, the wife of the seventh Earl of Cork was a popular society figure, well known for her parties and her friendships with the leading lights of the day. Lord Byron, Dr Johnson and the Prince of Wales were just a few of the famous people who attended her soirées.

She was still playing the hostess well into her 90s, and maintained some rather strange idiosyncracies, which Charles Dickens would later use when describing some of the peculiarities of Mrs Hunter in The Pickwick Papers. One of which was the rather odd way her drawing rooms were arranged. There were no tables, just rows upon rows of armchairs , all with their backs facing the wall. And if you think that was slightly odd, all the chairs had also been screwed to the floor so they were impossible to move.

Despite being a wonderful hostess, her party invitations were rarely reciprocated. This was due to another of her odd traits: she was a kleptomaniac. When Lady Cork went shopping, shop keepers would never allow their goods to be taken to her carriage for approval, as was the custom with people of wealth and position. They always insisted that she went into the shop and, once there, an assistant was appointed to follow her whilst she was browsing. On the increasingly rare occasions she was invited to other peoples homes, the servants were instructed to remove all of their finest silver and replace them with pewter or tin. This seemed to have no effect on our light-fingered aristocrat, as she would nonchalantly pick them up and secrete them in her muff as she left. Upon her return home her servants (well used to her proclivities) would gather up the booty and send it back to the owners with an apology. She once took a fancy to another guest's carriage and instructed her driver to make off with it. The owner eventually turned up after a couple of days to reclaim his carriage and no doubt expecting to receive an explanation and apology. Instead he was subjected to a litany of complaints from Lady

Cork: the seats were uncomfortable and the steps of the carriage were too high for her short legs.

And of course there is the famous story of when she was so obviously unimpressed with the quality of silver on offer that she decided to liberate a live hedgehog, which she popped in her handbag whilst she was saying goodbye to her hosts.

MOSS KEANE (1948-2010)

Maurice Ignatius Keane was a giant of Irish rugby between 1974 and 1984, during which time he played in fifty-one Internationals. He was a tireless forward, and, as the late rugby commentator Bill McClaren once memorably said before a game against England, he was 'eighteen and a half stone of prime Irish beef on the hoof. I don't know about the opposition but he frightens the living daylights out of me.'

There is a lovely story involving the mighty All Blacks, when they came to Landsdowne Road in 1978. Struggling to stay in the match, the Irish were consistently second best in the line-outs and realised that their only chance of success was to try and confuse the New Zealanders with an extremely complex series of line-out calls. However, the visitors received help from an unexpected source, when, following one very long line-out call from the Irish hooker, they heard Keane shout 'Oh, God, not to me again!'

A man well known for his wit, he had a fund of stories (sadly most of them unprintable). But there is one story worthy of mention. A few days before the match against Wales, anxious to build his strength up, he went to the butchers and asked for a pig's head. When the butcher asked where he should cut it, Keane replied, 'As close to the arse as possible.'

EDWARD EYRE (1753-98)

The delightfully dotty Ned Eyre lived in Carrick-on-Suir in County Waterford with his 'daughters and heiresses', Miss Dapper and Miss Kitsey, who were two spotted Labradors.

He was very particular about his appearance. He would wear the brightest coloured silks and satins, always with a fur lining. His shoes would be in a matching satin with large silver buckles. To top off his ensemble he would carry a fan or a muff (depending on the weather) and would apply so much makeup that he resembled an eighteenth-century Boy George. His cousin, Dorothea Herbert, recalled one occasion in 1782 when he attended the races wearing a pink suit covered in dia-manté buttons and what appeared to be a calfskin codpiece.

He kept very odd hours, rarely coming downstairs before noon, and he seemed to subsist solely on tea, sweetmeats and pickles. No doubt due to his love affair with his wardrobe, he eventually ended up in debt and died in 1798. He was also prone to outbursts of great generosity: he would sometimes invite 'all the beggars of Galway' to his house for hot tea, toast and chocolate.

He had a cousin, a Colonel Giles Eyre, who also managed to run through a great fortune, but in a slightly more conventional manner. He was a great sportsman and kept fifty horses and over seventy dogs, but he too had a touch of eccentricity: he would leave coins in a big copper bowl outside his house so that beggars could help themselves.

In 1811, he decided to stand for Parliament in Galway. His opponent was a man called Richard Martin, a man of short temper and propensity for duelling who was also known as 'Hair Trigger Dick'. He offered not to oppose him if Eyre would simply sign some papers, but Eyre refused, as he was illiterate. So Eyre went to the polls. Despite having spent over £80,000, he still managed to lose the election. It was later discovered that the papers that Martin wanted him to sign were bills of sale for some properties that he had his eye on. Giles Eyre is commemorated in Charles Lever's ballad 'The Man from Galway', the chorus of which is 'With debts galore, but fun far more / Oh, that's the man from Galway'.

Lord Eyre from Eyrescourt, from whom Giles had inherited his fortune, was equally odd. He lived in a castle with windows that did not open, doors that would not close, and a vast library with no books; he burnt them all to keep warm. Another late riser, he would be found seated at his favourite table from early afternoon to late evening, working his way through vast amounts of meat and claret. The food, which never varied, was presented in such a manner to discourage guests: a slaughtered ox was hung up whole and diners were expected to help themselves.

BRENDAN BEHAN (1923-64)

The greatest Irish writer of his generation, who wrote the critically acclaimed *Borstal Boy* and *The Quare Fellow*, famously described himself as 'a drinker with a writing problem'.

He was raised on whiskey by his maternal grandmother because 'it was good for the worms'. This was also the same grandmother who, Behan claimed, would only get out of bed to go to funerals.

He achieved national notoriety with a series of drunken appearances on television, most memorably on a 1956 episode of BBC's *Panorama* when after mumbling through an interview he suddenly got up, stating, 'I have to take a leak', and did not return. He reprised this a few years later when he was a guest with the American actor Jackie Gleason on an American chat show, during which he didn't manage a single comprehensible word. Gleason described the incident by saying: 'It wasn't an act of God, it was an act of Guinness.'

Back in Ireland, Behan was contracted to write an advertising slogan for Guinness – now recognised as possibly one of the worst decisions ever made by an advertising agency. He was given half a dozen kegs of their product for inspiration. After a month the company asked the legendary writer what he had come up with. Behan replied, 'Guinness makes you drunk.'

There is also that famous story of when he was visiting Canada in 1961 and was asked by a reporter, 'What brings you to Canada, Mr Behan?' Behan is supposed to have replied, 'Well now, I was in a bar in Dublin and it had one of those signs, and it said "Drink Canada Dry", so I thought I'd give it a shot.'

He was also in the habit of interrupting his own plays. One night he yelled out, 'That's not what I wrote!' and then clambered on to the stage, only to discover he was in the wrong theatre, watching a totally different play.

When he was not 'in his cups' he was a very witty man. On being asked by a journalist to describe the difference between poetry and prose, he replied:

There was a young man named Rollocks,
who worked for Ferrier Pollocks.
As he walked on the Strand.
With his girl by the hand.
The tide came up to his knees.

'Now that's prose,' he said. 'If the tide had been in, it would have been poetry.'

His love of the bottle finally claimed him on 8 March 1964, when he collapsed at the Harbour Lights bar in Dublin, and died a few days later, aged 41.

BRIAN MAGUIRE (1770-1835)

Brian Maguire was perhaps the greatest duellist of his time in Ireland.

He started life as a junior officer in the East India Company where he appeared to be a quiet and unassuming man, until an event took place that shaped the rest of his life. While on duty at Cochin (a seaport on the Malabar coast) a Captain Thurling took umbrage at Maguire's success with the very limited supply of ladies and challenged him to a duel. The match was somewhat unequal, as Maguire chose to face the captain's sword with only a billiard cue – however, he escaped unscathed and Thurling was fatally wounded. Having cleared his name, Maguire found that there was no turning back: he became addicted to duelling.

His return to Dublin and subsequent marriage did little to dampen his ardour. Indeed his wife, who perhaps should have been more of a pacifying influence on him, assisted him by holding – at arm's length – the lighted candle he used for target practice.

When he required the attendance of a servant he had a rather novel way of ringing the bell. His pistols always lay on the table beside him, and, instead of simply ringing the bell he took up a pistol and fired it at the handle of the bell, and continued firing till he hit it, thus making the bell ring.

As his reputation as a bona fide lunatic increased, he was faced with a shortage of possible opponents. But the resourceful fellow remedied this by leaning out of the window and emptying his chamber pot on passersby. When they looked up, he spat on them and immediately offered them the opportunity of settling the matter on the field of honour. Incredibly, he was never arrested or prosecuted for this behaviour.

A long and ultimately fruitless court case for the recovery of his wife's fortune led to Maguire's eventual impoverishment. When his eldest son, George, died at the age of 12 in 1830, Maguire, using techniques he had learned in India, embalmed him himself. He kept the mummified young George in a glass case that went everywhere with him until his own death five years later.

CHARLES MATURIN (1782-1824)

The Reverend Charles Maturin was obsessed with dancing. He would dance at any opportunity and he quickly wore out his wife with his impromptu dancing sessions. Keen to carry on, with or without his wife, he then organised morning quadrille parties at his friend's houses and, at least three times a week, pranced about on their carpets until they were all threadbare.

A lithe, athletic man, he was always keen to show off his fine figure. He favoured a huge greatcoat tossed gracefully over his shoulders and tight pantaloons to display his legs. He wore net stockings and evening clothes even when fishing.

He soon found that a curate's stipend did not allow for his exotic tastes so, faced with potential financial embarrassment, he began to write. Romantic novels with titles like *Fatal Revenge* and *The Wild Irish Boy* flowed from his pen, followed by a succession of lurid Gothic novels that proved to be remarkably popular. The money he received he tended to spend flamboyantly. He spent heavily on the most fashionable of clothes and he had the ceiling of his house in Dublin painted with scenes from his novels.

Despite his success as a writer, he always seemed to be on the verge of bankruptcy. Even when funds were low he insisted that his wife should always be beautifully groomed; he wished her to wear layer upon layer of rouge and often ordered her back to her dressing table to apply a thicker application.

He enjoyed company whilst he was working, but would stick a Holy Communion wafer on his forehead as a sign that he was not to be disturbed. He would also make sure that he would not join in any conversation by covering his mouth with a paste made of bread and water.

As he got older he became more and more absent-minded. He often made social calls in his dressing gown and slippers, or went out wearing one shoe and one boot. He loved parties, but was likely to turn up a day early or late. He sent his great novel, *Melmoth the Wanderer*, to his publishers as a stack of several thousand out-of-order and unnumbered pages.

He was only 42 when he died in 1824. His end was hastened due to his continued absent-mindedness, as he died due to having taken the wrong medicine.

VALENTINE BROWNE (1891-1943)

Valentine Browne, originally from Mount Browne, County Limerick, had his elbow shot away during the First World War and, as a result of this injury, spent the rest of his days carrying the damaged arm at a most peculiar angle to his body.

He owned a vast collection of fishing rods, which he would buy from a shop in Dublin. Whenever he called in to make a potential purchase, the shop assistant was required to carry armfuls of the rods to the kerbside, where he would make practice casts into the traffic.

He once took 400 books with him on a ten-day cruise but did not read any of them. He was also an erratic but keen golfer and one day at a local auction decided to buy a job lot of 147 golf clubs. Whenever he found himself in a bunker he would drop to his knees and pray. Once, whilst playing a round at Lahinch golf club in County Clare, he hit a particularly wayward shot and found himself in a bunker with a particularly difficult lie. After kneeling in the sand for a full five minutes, he then rose and added before playing his shot, 'but don't send Jesus, this is no job for a boy.'

HARRY BADGER

Dressed in a red military-style tunic and his yellow buckskin trousers, he became a well-known figure in Cork during the early 1800s. He would wander up and sit down near the old courthouse in South Main Street and while away the hours by smoking his pipe.

Constantly being teased by children, he took to wearing a brass helmet covered in iron spikes to protect his head from all the objects that were thrown at him.

He was renowned for his complete indifference to what he ate or drank. He could and would eat or drink anything that was put in front of him. This inevitably prompted an endless stream of wagers on how far he could be persuaded to go. On one occasion someone dropped a mouse into his pint of porter. Harry saw it, ignored it and calmly finished his drink. When asked if he had seen anything odd in his porter, he replied 'so I did – a fly'. His last meal was a bowl of 'tripe', which was in fact strips taken from an old pair of leather breeches, boiled and served with a milk and honey sauce. It took him two days to eat it. On the third day he died.

He was so popular that many artists sketched him and some of their portraits were reproduced on tin and used as chimney ornaments.

JAMES USSHER (1581-1656)

James Ussher was a seventeenth-century Archbishop of Armagh who wanted to calculate the age of the world. So one day, sometime in 1648, he sat down and very slowly and rather carefully began counting all the 'begats' in the Old Testament. When he had finally finished in 1650, Ussher then published his book with the snappy title of *Annales veteris testamenti, a prima mundi origine deducti* (Annals of the Old Testament, deduced from the earliest Beginning of the World).

In this weighty tome he had painstakingly reconstructed the history of the world based on the Bible, Egyptian and Jewish chronologies. To the delight of all future academics he needed over 12,000 footnotes to reference all the secular sources and 2,000 footnotes for all of the religious sources.

The world, he finally concluded, had begun one weekend in 4004 BC, or to be more precise, at around 6 p.m. on Saturday, 22 October. This started a feeding frenzy among the scholars of the day, who were all anxious to perform their own calculations and there were many earnest debates about whether time would have begun on the Saturday evening or the Sunday morning. Ussher chose 23 October for his moment of Creation as it was the date of the autumn equinox, which for many people was seen as the traditional start to the year. Ussher then surmised that the 23rd would have obviously had to have been a Sunday as per 'and He rested on the seventh day.... etc.'

When it came to the printing of English Bibles and adding a chronology in the margins, Ussher's calculation was the one chosen, and until the late 1970s all the Gideon Bibles found in hotel rooms still carried his dating system.

SAMUEL BOYCE (1701-42)

Born in Dublin in 1701, Boyce was the epitome of laziness. He frequently did not attend school for months at a time, only to turn up for exams, which he invariably passed with flying colours. Instead of going to Trinity he chose to attend Glasgow University, where he then married a barmaid and decided that he would not take up a career but would become a poet. Living off his new wife's meagre salary, he quickly ran out of money and, leaving behind a trail of unpaid bills, he decided to return to Dublin. He then spent a few years living off his father. But when his father died, he was left a small inheritance, and so Boyce decided to return to Scotland and this time make his name as a poet.

After writing a rather sweet elegy in 1736, *The Tears of the Muses: A Poem Sacred to the Memory of the Right Honourable Anne, late Viscountess of Stormont*, mourning the death of Viscountess Stormont, he was offered a well-paid position in the Customs Office by her grateful husband. It happened to be raining on the day of his new job, so Boyce decided to stay in bed and not bother turning up in case he got wet.

He was constantly borrowing money to redeem his clothes from various pawnshops, but they were always back in pawn within a day. He would frequently, on receipt of some money following one of his begging letters, go on a binge and spend the lot on fine food and rich wines, whilst his poor wife was left starving at home. When the begging letters failed, he would resort to subterfuge, seeking payment for poems that he had never written. One summer, down on his luck (again), he hatched a cunning ploy. He sent his wife out to tell all and sundry that he was dead, in the hope that he would receive a widow's pension. It did not go well, as on the evening of his 'death' he was found drinking in his local tavern.

During the many, many times when his clothes had been pawned and he did not have the money to redeem them, he would spend all day in bed covered by a single blanket. If he felt like writing a poem, he would sit up in bed with the paper on his knee and the blanket wrapped around him. He would then write his poem through a previously cut hole just large enough for him to poke his writing arm through.

He even invented a paper collar and shirt, consisting of strips of paper at his neck and wrists. Wearing a coat over this arrangement, but no trousers (he did not possess any), he sometimes visited friends, much to the distress of any ladies who were present.

When his wife died in 1745, Boyce had no money for mourning clothes, so he brought a piece of black ribbon for his dog to wear.

When he finally died at the age of 41, he had alienated just about everybody he knew and was buried in a pauper's grave, as no one felt inclined to pay for his funeral.

FINBAR NOLAN (1952-)

Finbar Nolan is seen by some to be the most successful Irish healer since the wonderfully strange Valentine Greatrakes in the seventeenth century.

According to the people who know about such things, if you are the seventh son of a seventh son you are able, and apparently obliged, to cure things such as eczema and asthma. Nolan, who has the requisite number of brothers and uncles, has been treating far more impressive diseases. He started his healing whilst still in nappies, when he laid his hands on another child and the toddler was subsequently cured of ringworm.

Nolan believes that worms are responsible for rheumatism and arthritis – not the normal worm you see in the garden, but a special worm which lives in the spine. The not particularly scientific reason for this was because of an event that happened when he was a young child. His mother, for some reason, decided to put a worm in his hand, and apparently the worm just shrivelled up and died. When he appeared on television a few years ago, he was asked about this claim and was given three worms to hold. He closed his fist, and then slowly opened it, the camera zoomed in … to focus on three very much alive and still wriggling worms.

It appeared to have done no harm to his reputation, as there are still queues of people willing to stand in line outside his home in County Cavan for the laying on of hands. He does not charge anything for his services, but grateful patients are not discouraged from leaving a donation in an envelope.

JOHN MCAULEY (1867-C. 1912)

The Irish rugby team of 1887 contained the Limerick forward John Macauley. He had been selected to play in the game against England but was dismayed to discover that he had used up all his annual leave from work. A quick glance at his conditions of employment revealed that the only circumstances in which he could be granted additional leave was for a honeymoon. So, without a moment's hesitation, he proposed to his girlfriend and fixed the wedding date for the morning of the match. At the conclusion of the nuptials, Macauley and his bride raced to the ground in time for him to take his place in the Irish line-up. It seems that the union was blessed, as Ireland ran out as winners of the game.

JOHN BARRETT (1753-1821)

Barrett was a vice-provost and professor of Classics at Trinity College, Dublin. One of the brightest minds of his generation, he spoke and wrote Latin and Greek fluently, but seemed to have difficulty making himself understood in English. In the words of a contemporary, Barrett was 'so ignorant of his own (language) that his conversation was a tissue of blunders and grammatical absurdities'.

Barrett's lectures were extremely popular, not so much due to his extraordinary intellect but more to his curious habit of swearing at the end of every sentence.

Learned as he was in certain matters academic, Barrett was almost unbelievably ignorant when it came to everyday life. Leaving home at 14, he entered Trinity in 1767 as a student and then lived the rest of his life behind its walls, only leaving the university three times a year – once for the Fellows annual outing and twice to the Bank of Ireland to collect his dividends.

There is a famous story of him looking out of a window and asking what type of animal was grazing. He was delighted to discover that he was looking at 'live mutton' (sheep). He was equally confused when it came to women. One evening at a Fellows dinner, glasses were raised 'to the health of the ladies'. The Master of College asked Barrett to propose his 'belle' – he apparently replied 'I'll give you the college bell. For I'm told she's finer than Big Tom of Lincoln.'

He was also well known for his inability to apply simple logic to everyday situations. There is the story of when a visiting clergyman asked him why he had two holes at the bottom of his door.

'To let the cats in and out,' Barrett replied.

'Surely,' said his visitor, 'would not one do for both?'

'You silly man, how could the big cat go through the small hole?' replied Barrett.

'But could not the little one go through the big hole?'

'Egad,' said the doctor, 'and so she could, but I never thought of that!'

Barrett was good-natured but not generous with money. He lived frugally, supplementing his income by collecting and selling old candle ends. However, rather than go to the expense of a fire in his room, Barrett would frequently sneak down to the kitchens and warm himself in front of the kitchen fire. Another of his money-saving tips was to powder his own hair, instead of buying a wig. Every evening he would carefully comb the powder out of his hair onto a sheet of paper and save it for when he would need it again.

He always dined in the Hall because it was free, and during the course of the day would budget himself to just a halfpenny's worth each of bread and milk. These were fetched for him by his faithful servant, Catty. One day, however, she slipped and injured herself quite badly and was taken to hospital. On hearing news of her mishap Barrett rushed over to see her.

After expressing his sympathy and asking how she felt, he then asked, 'D'ye hear, Catty, where's the jug?'

'Oh, doctor, sure the jug was broke when I fell.'

'Very good, Catty, that can't be helped; but d'ye see me now, where's my halfpenny change?'

He died in 1821 and left the enormous sum of £80,000 – 'to feed the hungry and clothe the naked'.

COLONEL CECIL BROWN LECKIE

In the summer of 1925 in Greencastle, County Donegal, Colonel Leckie's dog died. It was an elderly spaniel called Peter. The Colonel was so distraught that he sent all his servants away and went into a period of mourning for a month. During this time he designed a specially lined and padded coffin in the shape of a dog. It was into this that poor Peter's remains were placed. There was then a procession around the village, in which the odd-shaped coffin was borne on the shoulders of his servants, with the Colonel walking behind them. The funeral cortege eventually ended up at the estate's churchyard, where Peter was buried in the family vault. The colonel then had the following inscription placed on a brass plate on the dog's coffin:

> In memory of Peter a faithful dog and friend to Colonel Brown Leckie DLJP.
> Such was my dog who now without my aid
> Hunts through the shadowland, himself a shade
> Or crouched perchance before some ghostly gate
> Awaits my step as here he used to wait.

The Colonel made sure that Peter's coffin was placed in such a way that, when he eventually died, Peter would be lying at his feet. Just over a year later the colonel did indeed die and he was laid to rest in the family vault, reunited with his faithful hound.

JOHN HOWARD TAYLOR (1904-69)

Dublin-born John Howard Taylor, an adventurer by trade, spent over thirty years in Africa as a professional big game hunter. He claimed that he had killed over 1,000 elephants.

He would frequently be out of touch with civilisation, sometimes for as long as a year. Indeed he was blissfully unaware of the outbreak of the Second World War until some of his men brought back provisions from a remote trading post,wrapped in some old newspapers. Upon reading these he discovered that Europe was at war.

When he finally returned to Ireland, the only clothes he seemed to wear were his old safari outfits, complete with his large white hat and a much-battered machete tucked into his waistband. He was also in the habit of practising what he called 'camouflaging techniques' by hiding in the bushes of the various parks around the city, and then jumping out and startling anyone who was passing by.

CORMAC MACDONLEVY

MacDonlevy was an Irish physician of the fifteenth century, and was responsible for the advancement of Irish medicine by translating European medical texts from Latin into the vernacular. Most laudable, I am sure you will agree. But it led to some most peculiar and eccentric cures.

Take for example, contraception. MacDonlevy, following the latest advice of the day, would have suggested pouring pepper into the mouth of the uterus. This seems to have been an early forerunner of complementary medicine, as sneezing is not a bad way of expelling semen from the vagina. He also recommended only having sex during the first five days after menstruation, a method which became known as 'Vatican roulette'.

One of the many books he translated was a textbook called *De Urinas*, which prompted the new vogue of uroscopy. Macdonlevy was responsible for the sudden appearance of 'pisse-prophets', who would indulge in 'urine gazing' – making detailed diagnoses from the colour, smell and even taste of the patient's urine.

Like many of his ilk, MacDonlevy also actively sought to lower the libido and suggested applying daisies to the genitals. But his weirdest remedy must surely have been the application of burnt feathers and horse dung as a cure for haemorrhoids.

FRANCIS JACK NEEDHAM, EARL OF KILMOREY (1787-1880)

This is a story about a building, a building that was moved. That in itself is not unusual, as large structures do sometimes move location – for example the old London Bridge was transported to Arizona. But there is something extraordinary about a building being moved not once but three times; over a twelve-year period, this is exactly what the nutty Earl of Kilmorey did. The building in question was a highly decorated Egyptian mausoleum that he had built in the grounds of Orleans House, his London residence, for his mistress, Priscilla Anne Hoste.

Kilmorey seemed to have permanently itchy feet. In Ireland, home was a 55,000-acre estate at Mourne Park but, like a one man version of RTE's *Find Me a Home*, he is recorded as buying and selling houses on an almost yearly basis. Little surprise, then, that before long he had lost interest in Orleans House and moved to Woburn Park in Weybridge, Surrey, taking the mausoleum with him so it could be rebuilt close by.

That was in 1862. But within six years, Kilmorey was off again, this time back to Twickenham and Gordon House which, whether he remembered or not, he had previously owned back in the early 1850s. Once more, the mausoleum was dismantled, moved and re-erected, but this time it was for good.

His other eccentricities included a refusal to wear socks, as he was convinced that they were bad for his circulation, and sleeping in a coffin during the summer and having his man wheel him back and forth to the mausoleum whilst he lay in the box, trying it out for size.

When he finally died, the Earl was laid to rest next to his beloved Priscilla, wearing a dressing gown fashioned from rat's fur.

LOLA MONTEZ (1821-61)

Lola Montez, born Eliza Gilbert in Grange, County Sligo in 1821, led a life that shocked the world, yet died (apparently) repentant, in the bosom of the church.

Lola first came to public notice when, aged only 15 and still at school, she fell for the charms of an army officer home on leave, to whom she was hastily married by her horrified mother. The girl returned to India with her new husband but, finding life there appallingly dreary, soon embarked on an affair that led him to sue for divorce.

On returning to London, with no money and no immediate prospects, she reinvented herself as a 'Spanish' exotic dancer named Lola Montez. Her 'Spider Dance', which started riots among the male audiences of the day, involved her playing the part of a peasant girl who discovers that a tarantula has crept into her clothing. She would strut to the footlights, lift each one of her many coloured petticoats, shake imaginary spiders free and then step on them, flashing her legs and underwear (frequently missing). She was condemned by society, but there was no other act quite like it in the world.

There is, however, no disputing Montez's claim to have been one of the leading beauties of the age, and in 1846, while touring Germany, she was asked to pose for a portrait that would be hung in the fabled 'Gallery of Beauties' commissioned by Ludwig, King of Bavaria. Ludwig promptly fell in love with her and installed her as his mistress, eventually falling so fully for her charms that she became the de facto ruler of his kingdom until 1848, a year of revolution in Europe. Lola's numerous enemies then took advantage of the tense political climate to hound her from Bavaria.

She returned to the stage, hiring a troupe of dancers and touring with them extensively throughout the world. She created a sensation in California at the time of the Gold Rush, where she publically horsewhipped a lover who had enraged her.

Her temper was legendary: the composer Franz Listz, as he left Lola sleeping in their hotel room in Paris, paid the bill and left a stack of banknotes to the manager explaining, 'This should cover the cost of the furniture, when she wakes up and discovers I have left.'

In her late 30s, Montez returned to the United States, where, as her beauty faded, an apparently genuine religious conversion took place that led her back to the church where she became involved in various charitable causes.

Montez published a number of books about her life including *Anecdotes of Love; Being a True Account of the Most Remarkable Events Connected with the History of Love; in All Ages and among All Nations* (1858), *The Arts of Beauty, or, Secrets of a Lady's Toilet with Hints to Gentlemen on the Art of Fascination* (1858), and *Lectures of Lola Montez, Including Her Autobiography* (1858).

After an argument with an over-persistent suitor following a late-night supper, she refused the offer of a taxi and walked home in the rain. She died a couple of weeks later, a month shy of her 40th birthday, of pneumonia.

BUCK WHALEY (1766-1800)

When his father died in 1780, the young Buck Whaley inherited an estate in County Wicklow with the rather substantial income of £7,000 a year. Even at a young age Whaley was showing the rakish and libertine characteristics that would follow him through his life.

His despairing family sent him to Paris in 1782 in an attempt to educate him as a gentleman. This had the complete opposite effect – free from the strictures of Irish society he wholeheartedly embraced the seedy underbelly of Paris with all its attendant offerings. It did not end well, however; after losing £10,000 in one evening, he had to flee back to Ireland when his cheque bounced.

On his return to Dublin he was already getting a reputation as a scoundrel, but one evening in a tavern came the moment that would change his life. Whilst regaling his friends with stories of his time in Paris, he was asked where he would go next. He replied Jerusalem. His fellow bucks then wagered £15,000 that he would not be able to reach Jerusalem and return with a letter proving it within a period of two years.

In the autumn of 1788, the intrepid Whaley set sail. He eventually returned in June 1789 – clutching a signed document from a convent in Jerusalem proving that his visit had taken place. His triumph was recorded in the popular song at the time 'Round the World for Sport'.

Flushed with success (and the £15,000 winnings) he then went through a stage of taking ridiculous wagers, one of which involved him jumping from his drawing room window, into the first passing carriage and kissing its occupant. He also conceived a plan to save Louis XVI from the guillotine, but got so drunk on the voyage to France that he promptly turned round and went home. Other wacky wagers included the time he managed to lose 150 guineas to the future Duke of Wellington in a bet on how far Whaley could walk in a day.

A most peculiar man in many ways, he once went down on one knee to propose to a young woman who had stopped in front of his house to check her bonnet in the window.

But his longstanding love affair with the card table steadily worsened and in order to pay his creditors he not only took bribes to vote for the union with Britain, but he also took further bribes to vote against it. Despite this, he still managed to accumulate more debts and finally had to flee to the Isle of Man.

Determined to win yet another bet, this time 'to live on Irish soil without being in Ireland', he imported soil from Ireland for the foundations of the new house. However, the house was never built, as Whaley died of rheumatic fever on 2 November 1800.

In the final years of his life he had started to write his memoirs, in which he stated, 'my extraordinary levities proceeded, not from a corrupted heart, but an eccentric and exalted imagination and ridiculous pretensions to notoriety.'

Eccentric to the end, he wrote in his will that he wanted 'a Mr Robinson, an Irishman, to dance a hornpipe over the coffin'.

ARTHUR KAVANAGH (1831-89)

Born with only the rudiments of arms and legs at Borris House, County Carlow, life looked decidedly bleak for Arthur Kavanagh. But the young boy refused to let these impediments hold him back. He quickly learned to ride horses by being strapped to a special saddle and guiding the horse with a special set of reins.

In 1849, Kavanagh's mother discovered that the naughty boy had been having his way with a number of girls on the family estate, so she sent him into exile to Uppsala in India. He then travelled all across Egypt and Persia, although whilst in Persia his request for more funds was denied when his mother found out that he had spent a whole month in a harem.

This extraordinary fellow became not only an MP but also a Privy Councillor, and a more than proficient watercolour painter. During his travels across India he also gained a reputation as being a fine shot whilst hunting tigers.

He married in 1855 and fathered seven healthy children. He was a much-loved local character and wonderfully unselfconscious. He exclaimed to one of his friends on a trip to Waterford, 'It's an extraordinary thing – I haven't been here in five years but the stationmaster still recognised me!'

Arthur Kavanagh died of pneumonia on 25 December 1889 and was buried in Ballicopagan Cemetery, Carlow.

EKUNDAYO O'BADMUS

According to *The Sun* (so it must be true), the multiple winner of the Irish Monopoly Championship, Ekundayo Badmus, changed his name by deed poll in order to represent Ireland in the Monopoly World Championships of 2009. He is now known as Ekundayo O'Badmus.

DANIEL O'CONNELL (1775-1847)

Known as the Liberator, Daniel O'Conell is now seen as a national treasure due to his tireless campaigning for Catholic emancipation. There was, however, a darker side to him – he killed a man in a duel.

Renowned for his fiery oratory, he appeared to have over stepped the mark when after calling the Dublin Corporation 'beggarly' he refused to apologise. One of the members of the Dublin Corporation, a well-known duellist called John D'Esterre thus challenged him to a duel. Bearing in mind the politics of the time and the British government's view that O'Connell was 'worse than a public nuisance', the duel was no doubt encouraged by the authorities. At 3.00 a.m. sometime in early February 1815, at Bishops Court in County Kildare, the two men finally met. D'Esterre missed with his shot but O'Connell did not, fatally wounding D'Esterre in the stomach.

Far from enjoying his success, it seems O'Connell was plagued by guilt. He later offered D'Esterre's young widow a share of his annual salary, which she refused. However, many years later she was the subject of a lawsuit over some land in Cork, and upon hearing this O'Connell made his way to the court and successfully represented her.

For the rest of his life, if he ever had occasion to pass D'Esterre's house, he would stop, take his hat off and bless himself. This feeling of guilt also occurred when he would attend Mass. He had an eccentric habit of wearing a single black glove, which he believed would spare God from seeing the hand that fired that fateful shot.

SIR WILLIAM ARBUTHNOT LANE (1856-1943)

There have been many medical fads throughout the years, but without doubt one of the silliest was one man's obsession with removing people's colons. The man responsible was the extraordinarily bad-tempered Scots-Irish surgeon Sir William Butler Lane. This conqueror of colons was the resident surgeon at Guy's Hospital in London.

Lane had a number of eccentric theories on how to treat the colon. One of his suggestions was a daily enema using a pint of cream, and another was to always sleep on your back. His wacky research also came to the conclusion that red-haired, particularly Irish, women were naturally immune to constipation.

His obsession with the colon reached its peak in 1903. He had written an article in which he suggested that the colon was completely redundant to the requirements of the human body. It was merely a useless tube of tissue full of foul smells. Lane had finally found his mission in life – to rid the world of colons. He also argued that the humble colon was responsible for the incubation of a whole range of diseases, including cancer and tuberculosis. No colon was safe from Lane; even patients who came to see him for minor ailments would have their colon removed.

His one-man rectal campaign came to a halt after a few years when fellow doctors, finally taking notice that none of Lane's patients ever really benefited from their loss, took a more studied look at his theory and discovered it to be completely baseless.

You will no doubt be unsurprised to hear that Lane lived out the rest of his life in an asylum, where he died, discredited, aged 86.

RICHARD POCKRICH (1695-1759)

Richard Pockrich was born around 1695 and came from Aghnamallagh, County Monaghan. He was the oldest son of Richard Pockerich, an Irish landowner. His father died when he was 25, and he then inherited his father's estate, which came with an annual income of £4,000 – a staggering half a million pounds, in today's money.

Young Pockrich always thought of himself as a visionary and spent the rest of his life, and all of his fortune, dreaming up some of the most wonderfully hare-brained schemes that Ireland had ever seen.

His first attempt at a business was to turn the Bishop of Tuam's residence into a coffee house. Unsurprisingly the project was dropped when the somewhat baffled Bishop refused to move.

He then decided to set up a brewery in Islandbridge, but got so bored waiting for the building to be constructed that he quickly proceeded to his next venture: geese. Pockrich was convinced that he could make Ireland the main geese supplier for the whole of Europe. He then spent the best part of a year buying up swathes of land (much to the delight of grateful farmers) all across the Wicklow mountains in order to build the biggest goose farm in Ireland. Sadly, this particular project was also doomed to failure, when he belatedly discovered that the Wicklow mountains was no place to breed geese.

Other fanciful notions were a proposal to parliament that all the bogs in Ireland should be drained and used as vineyards and, perhaps the nuttiest suggestion of all, manufacturing wings for people. He believed that his engineering skills (nil) harnessed with his shining intellect (doubtful) would allow him to build wings that would mean 'the men and women of Ireland would never have to walk anywhere again.'

He also tabled a proposal outlining how eternal life could be achieved using blood transfusions. Pockrich was aware of the potential complications if death was no longer an issue for everyone. So, with the same sense of intensity and commitment he had applied to all of his previous enterprises, he suggested a new Act of Parliament, which would ensure that anyone 'attaining to an age of 999 years to be for all intents and purpose dead in law'. He quite reasonably argued that this would allow relatives to claim their inheritances and, if necessary, priests to go to court to claim burial fees from legally dead 999-year-old parishioners.

However, there were occasions when some of his plans seemed to be inspired. In fact, he was described by one of his contemporaries as a 'man of amazing ingenuity employed in a hundred different schemes and inventions'.

He was an early advocate of a kind of FAS scheme to help the unemployed. He spoke and wrote about the need for canals to connect the Shannon with the Liffey, many years before it was officially mooted, and perhaps his most prescient moment was when he proposed that ships should be built with metal hulls rather than the traditional wooden ones. This in itself is quite remarkable, considering it would be another hundred years or so before the first one would be built.

In between his 'schemes' he twice ran for parliament (to no avail) after being told to do so by 'the ghost of a dead hag' who appeared to him at his ill-fated goose farm in the Wicklow mountains.

But there was one thing that he would have been justifiably proud of: his angelic organ. This device consisted of a number of glasses of different sizes filled with varying amounts of water and was 'played' by running a damp finger around the rim. There is a tale of two bailiffs who came to arrest the by now impoverished Pockrich; after seeing him play the angelic organ, the story goes, they were so moved that they left in tears without making the arrest. News of this remarkable musical instrument quickly spread and a tour was arranged for him. Unfortunately, on the very first leg of the tour at a concert hall in Dublin, just as he was starting, 'a large, unmannerly sow' made her way into the concert rooms, crapped all over the floor and shattered most of the angelic glasses. However, all was not lost, as the London debut in the following year 1744 was a great success. At last it seemed that fame and fortune was finally coming Pockrich's way and popular composers of the day wrote music specifically for the musical glasses.

Shortly after this uncharacteristic success, Pockerich returned to form by marrying a woman who, after eight years of running up dressmakers' bills, left him for another man. But the plucky Pokerich soldiered on, again standing unsuccessfully for the Irish parliament. He also started putting together plans for the disposal of his body after death. He instructed his executors to preserve his corpse in rum for the benefit of the public, 'who would be allowed to gaze upon the remains of this most remarkable person'.

In 1759 Pockerich died in a fire at a coffee house, when he insisted upon returning to the burning building in order to retrieve papers containing details of his next invention.

RICHARD BARRY, 7TH EARL OF BARRYMORE (1769-93)

Deep in the bowels of the British Library in London, you will find, amongst other things, the Reverend Daniel Lyson's *Collectiana*. These are scrapbooks of newspapers and hand-bills detailing the more colourful side of eighteenth-century London and Dublin. The good reverend seemed to have had a keen eye for the more bizarre goings on of the age.

Among the more startling items pasted into the scrapbooks are a collection of articles and letters regarding a 'most disagreeable wager' by the Irish rake Richard Barry, the 7th Earl of Barrymore, from County Cork.

On 13 March 1778 the following item appeared in *The World*:

> Amongst the curious bets of the day may be reckoned the following: The Duke of Bedford has betted a thousand guineas with Lord Barrymore that he does not eat a live cat. It is said His Lordship grounds his chances on having already made the experiment upon a kitten. The cat is to be fed as Lord Barrymore may choose.

This unusual bet attracted considerable public attention and several letters and articles appeared in subsequent issues of the newspaper, under the headline 'Cat-Eating'.

Barrymore later wrote to the newspaper to say its report had been mistaken. He had bet only that he could find a man who would eat a cat. But, despite this disclaimer, letters from self-appointed experts on competitive animal-eating continued to be printed. One of these had in 1777 seen an Irish man eat five fox cubs on a bet of £50 at a racecourse near Kildare, and observed that the bet of His Grace of Bedford that Lord Barrymore would not eat a live cat is not without precedence in the annals of sporting history.

Barrymore was popularly known as 'Hellgate' for his foul temper whilst drunk, while his sister Caroline was known as 'Billingsgate' because of her constant swearing. Henry, his younger brother, was known as 'Cripplegate' due to a deformity to one of his legs, and, to complete the full family set of nicknames, his youngest brother Augustus was called 'Newgate', as he had spent some time in that particular prison.

Barrymore died in the evening of 6 March 1793 at the age of 23, when his musket accidentally went off during a drinking session.

LADY MARGARET TYRELL (1890-1961)

Lady Margaret Tyrell was, by all accounts, a beautiful, highly intelligent and charming woman. Moving to Paris in 1934 as the wife of Lord Tyrell, the British ambassador to France, should have seen her playing the society hostess at all the many glittering galas and official functions. She was not, however, the typical diplomat's wife, and she was not particularly interested in doing any of those things; she spent most of her time at the British Library, researching her magnum opus: a book on the history of the world from 2000 bc to the present.

When she begrudgingly did visit Paris, the Dublin-born Lady Tyrell's favourite place to work was up a tree in the Embassy gardens. Here she would sit on a branch writing her book, and when she wished to summon a servant, she would blow one of the many whistles she kept around her neck. She had a different whistle for each servant.

In the evenings she would reluctantly attend the many Embassy receptions, where her natural charm and wit made up for such confusions as mistaking the future George VI for her husband's private secretary and spending the whole evening speaking French to Ramsey McDonald, the British Prime Minister, under the impression that he was the French Ambassador.

JOHN MCCONNELL

When the Irishman John McConnell arrived for his championship fight with Charley Davis for the English middleweight title in 1873, he discovered that he had forgotten to bring his bag of boxing gear. As a result of this oversight, there was a lengthy delay before the two boxers made their way to the ring.

After much rummaging around, some supposedly suitable garments were finally found. The large crowd could not believe their eyes when McConnell finally entered the ring, wearing an old pair of cricketing trousers that had been made for a man at least a foot shorter and about a foot wider.

Things were not looking good, and they got progressively worse. Whilst they were hunting for replacement shorts, the ice in McConnell's corner had melted. He spent the fight floundering around the ring trying to keep his trousers up while sweating heavily.

It was little wonder that the verdict went to his opponent.

JOHN TOLER (1745-1831)

The Nenagh-born judge John Toler was described by a contemporary as 'fat, pudgy, with small grey cunning eyes, which ever sparkled with good humour and irrepressible fun, especially when he was passing sentence of death'. Like the infamous Judge Jeffreys, he was without mercy and his sentences were harsh; he once sent ninety-seven men to their deaths in one day!

His courtroom manner was described as 'a combination of buffoonery and sadism', and he would combine drollery with a vicious dry wit. He would pass sentence by puffing his cheeks and quote poetry along with a very rambling speech. He would then throw his wig in the air to show that he had finished.

Astonishingly, Toler managed to remain a judge for twenty-seven years, despite the fact that, as the *Dictionary of National Biography* reported, 'his scanty knowledge of the law, his gross partiality, his callousness, and his buffoonery, completely disqualified him for the position.'

In the last few years before he retired in 1827, his behaviour got worse. He would fall asleep and snore loudly, before waking with a start and demand to know where he was.

Toler was famous for one single act of clemency towards an alleged murderer. Although the evidence against the accused was overwhelming, he recommended the jury to bring in a not guilty verdict, which caused a gasp of astonishment around the courtroom. The prosecutor interrupted the judge to remind him that the sheer weight of evidence showed the man's guilt was indisputable. Toler then replied testily, 'I realise that, but I hanged six men at last Tipperary Assizes who were innocent, so I'll let this man off to square matters.'

ROBERT COOK (1646-1726)

Farmer Robert Cook cut an unusual figure in seventeenth-century Ireland. He never wore anything but white linen, a sartorial eccentricity so well known that he became famous throughout Ireland as 'Linen Cook'. Not only were his underclothes, night clothes and shirts in purest white but so were his suits, coats and hats. At his farm in Cappoquin, County Waterford, he refused to have any black cattle and even his horses had to be the same pure white of his clothes.

He was a champion of animal rights, centuries before it became fashionable. Once, when a fox was caught attacking his chickens, Cook prevented his servants from killing it. Instead he gave the animal a stern lecture on the Fifth Commandment 'Thou shalt not kill' and sent it on its way.

Cook was extremely health-conscious, finding that 'water for drink and pulse, corn and other vegetatives for food, and linen and other vegetatives for raiment be quite sufficient'.

He died in 1726 when he was over 80 years old and was buried in, of course, a white linen shroud.

THOMAS DERMODY (1775-1802)

A poet, drunkard and perhaps the most ungrateful man of his generation, this erratic genius is now remembered more for his complete ingratitude to anyone who helped him, rather than for his poetry.

Born in Ennis, County Clare, Dermody was something of a child prodigy: he wrote some very well-received poems and was hailed by some as another Thomas Chatterton. A non-traditional path through life became apparent when he became an alcoholic by the age of 10, seemingly following in the footsteps of his father, a schoolmaster and lifelong drunk. By the age of 9 the precocious Dermody was helping his increasingly inebriated father to teach Latin and Greek. When he was 11, bored with the monotony of the classroom, he ran away from home, taking with him two shillings, a copy of Tom Jones and a spare shirt.

After arriving in Dublin, he wandered the streets for a while before taking shelter in a bookshop when it began to rain. Whilst poring over a Greek text, he met the first of his many soon-to-be-thoroughly-abused patrons, a Dr Houlton. Impressed with his knowledge of the classics, the good doctor brought him home and asked him to show off his knowledge for his friends in return for a roof over his head.

Quickly bored, he once again took to the streets. His next victim/mentor was an out-of-work theatrical set painter named Coyle. When the kind-hearted Coyle found him a job in a Dublin theatre, Dermody reluctantly agreed to help him paint scenery and generally help out. One day he read out a lampoon he had written on the rival merits of the two main actors playing at the theatre – one of whom, Robert Owenson, was so impressed with what he heard that he offered to buy the boy some new clothes and introduce him to his friends.

His benefactors included a veritable roll-call of the good and great – the likes of the Dowager Countess of Moira, Lord Kilwarden, the Attorney General , the Reverend Gilbert Austin, Henry Grattan and Henry Flood – and yet he treated each with disdain.

Having convinced a Mr. Boyd to put him through Trinity College, he left after a week, taking his tuition fees with him. Another, a certain Mr Tighe, mistook him for a beggar, thrashed him and then, realising his mistake, gave him a snuff box, a suit of clothes and a cocked hat. Inevitably everything ended up being pawned and the poet was once again forced to peddle his verses around the countryside in rags.

Desperate for money, having finally worn out his welcome with so many his previous patrons, Dermody then wrote to the Dowager Countess of Moira, whose kindness he had previously repaid with a savage essay entitled 'The Old Bachelors'. Lady Moira sent him half a crown, which prompted him to write the following: 'My Lady thank you for every former instance of your noble and generous favour. I cannot but wonder at receiving half a crown from a hand which has bestowed many guineas.'

Moving to London, he was taken up by some new patrons: a Mr Johnson, who presented him with a fashionable suit and a frilled shirt; and Sir James Bland Burgess, who helped him to obtain 10 guineas from a literary fund. Again, Dermody drank his good fortune away, and there was of course the recurring problem of his vanishing wardrobe. He had been given yet another suit by Sir James, but shortly afterwards he appeared at his house completely drunk and not wearing any trousers. Unsurprisingly, Sir James refused him any further help and sent him on his way.

Dermody then became ill with consumption and spent his last few years trying to stay one step ahead of his creditors before finally dying at the age of 27 in 1802.

SAMUEL DERRICK (1724-69)

Samuel Derrick, a Dublin-born would-be poet, was responsible for one of the best-selling books of the mid-eighteenth century. The fabulously named *A Catalogue of Jilts, Cracks & Prostitutes, Nightwalkers, Whores, She-Friends, Kind Women and other of the Linnen-lifting Tribe*. This 'must-have' book was a guide to the many distractions that a gentleman could pursue whilst out on the town, so to speak.

It gave explicit commentaries on the assets and characters of the ladies in question. To quote from its pages we find that Miss Smith, of Dukes Court in Bow Sreet is 'a well made lass, something under the middle size, with dark brown hair and a good complexion'. He gave a glowing report about a Mrs Hamblin of the Strand: 'the young lady in question is not above 56 ... we know she must be particularly useful to elderly gentleman who are very nice in having their linen got up'. Derrick then rhaposodises about a certain Mrs Dodd of Fleet Street who 'is reared on two pillars of monumental alabaster', and then praises a Mrs Clicamp of York Street for being 'one of the finest, fattest figures as fully furnished for fun and frolick ever formed ... fortunate for the true lovers of fat'. He did, however, point out that a Miss Dean should perhaps be avoided, as she displayed 'great indifference' to entertaining her client – cracking nuts while he was 'acting his joys'.

Derrick was originally apprenticed to a Dublin draper but quickly became disenchanted with the work and life in Dublin, and decided to reinvent himself as an Irish noble-man and left for London. Convinced of his talent as an actor, he managed to be cast in a couple of plays – which drew appalling reviews. Indeed, one critic wrote of him, 'Any other man might labour all his life and at last not get into so bad a method of playing.' Undeterred, and determined to become part of Dr Johnson's set, he took to following the great man around town and insinuating himself into various events. The few coins he had he tended to spend it on drink, and as a result he neglected his appearance to such an extent that he frequently resembled a tramp. The great Boswell, who recognised his awkward attempts at social climbing, described him as 'a little blackguard pimping dog'.

He also tried his hand at writing poetry, which was greeted with the same derision as his attempts at acting.

But when the Catalogue appeared, it seemed that the success that he sought had finally happened. Indeed, on hearing about the book, his only wealthy relative, an aunt in Dublin, became concerned about the attendant publicity and sent an emissary to London to ask him to desist. Derrick was away in Brighton on the day of the visit and the emissary was met by 'Mrs Derrick' – Jane Lessingham , an actress and prostitute who also received her own entry in his book. Needless to say, on receiving a report of the meeting the aunt promptly disinherited Derrick, and, to rub salt in his wounds, 'Mrs Derrick' then ran off with another man.

Nevertheless, the annual with its witty pen portraits of the women he knew so well sold in its thousands. Costing half a crown, which is equivalent to about £20 these days, it allowed him a few years sampling the life he had always craved – until he he had drunk his new-found wealth away and died in penury.

RICHARD CROSBIE (1755-1824)

The first Irishman ever to make a manned flight, Crosbie was a most peculiar-looking individual. Very tall and extremely thin, he was apparently 'more than a head over six feet' in height. On 19 January 1785, he took off in a hydrogen air balloon from Ranelagh gardens, on Dublin's southside and, after five minutes' flight, landed in Clontarf, on Dublin's northside.

The eccentric 30-year-old had even taken time to design what he later called his 'aerial dress'. This consisted of a very long robe of oiled silk with white fur trimmings, a waistcoat and breeches in a quilted white satin, a pair of shiny

Morocco boots for his feet, and for his head, a Montero cap of leopard skin with a white satin tassel. His balloon was embellished with paintings of Minerva, the Roman goddess of wisdom, and Mercury, the messenger of the gods, carrying the coat of arms of Ireland.

The day was somewhat tarnished by the Lord Mayor of Dublin, James Horan, who promptly banned hot air ballooning in Dublin declaring that 'too many Dubliners were spending their time gazing up at the sky instead of getting on with their work.'

Originally from Baltinglass, in County Wicklow, he had previously experimented with live animals as test pilots as he launched various prototype balloons in order to perfect the final design. One particular test flight involved a large ginger cat who ended up crash landing in the sea just off the coast of the Isle of Man. The poor old cat, who was wearing an address tag around its neck, was rescued by a fishing boat and was eventually returned to a no doubt delighted Crosbie.

His achievement in manned flight occurred just over a year after the Montgolfier Brothers did it in France. If Crosbie had spent a little less time on his 'aerial wardrobe' and more on his balloon, he probably would have beaten them to it.

SHANE MACGOWAN (1957-)

In order to demonstrate the 'cultural inferiority of the United States', the orthodontically-challenged Pogues lead singer once ate a Beach Boys album.

According to an article in the *Guardian*, 'he had become convinced (whilst off his head on acid) that the Third World War was taking place and that he, as the leader of the Irish Republic, was holding a summit meeting in his kitchen between the heads of state of the world superpowers: Russia, China, America and Ireland.'

The album in question? *The Beach Boys Greatest Hits, Volume 3.*

BANKER PATTERSON

Sometime in early December 1907, the Freeman's Journal, which was for a while the leading newspaper in Ireland, contained a rather curious report. Under its Recent Deaths column, it carried the news of the death of a 'Banker' Patterson. This in itself was not particularly newsworthy, but Patterson had left the quite astonishing sum of £90,000 to various charities.

You would have been given to believe that 'Banker' had either been a partner in one of the big financial houses or perhaps a wealthy merchant – none of the above, it would seem.

He was a different type of banker, as he seemed to have made his living as a moneylender. He would only lend a shilling but would insist on a penny per week in interest. By all accounts an extremely parsimonious individual, he once stole a jacket from a scarecrow and continued to wear it whatever the weather, and he would walk only on grass in order to preserve his shoe leather. He would also prefer to sit in the dark, in order not to buy a candle. And perhaps the most bizarre aspect of his miserliness was his refusal to wear trousers during the summer.

When he did die, his only possessions appeared to have been a cup, a dented tin plate and a knife with a broken handle and, of course, the aforementioned £90,000.

D.B. WALKINGTON (1867-1926)

D.B. Walkington was an Irish rugby player who represented his country eight times in the 1880s. He was so short sighted that he wore a monocle during matches and insisted on cleaning and polishing it before he attempted his kicks for goal.

Jacques McCarthy, the Irish rugby historian, commented: 'He is as good as can be on a bright day, but in the dark, his sight tells terribly against him.'

On the subject of rugby, although not strictly regarded as an eccentric, the late Mick English was responsible for one of the most famous quotes on the game. After English international Phil Horrocks-Taylor scored a dazzling try, he said: 'Every time I went to tackle him, Horrocks went one way, Taylor went the other and all I got was the f****** hyphen.'

RAY HEFFERNAN

Poor old Ray Heffernan of Cork City was branded Ireland's worst driver after failing the driving test for the fifteenth time in March 2017. Speaking on *The Neil Prendeville Show* on Cork FM, Mr Heffernan said he had been driving for fifty years and had never had an accident or a crash and had never been prosecuted for a road offence.

Whilst reviewing his fifteenth (and presumably not his last) test, the radio host went through the exam in detail with Mr Heffernan and found thirty-seven fails. These included his inability to stay in the right lane on the road, his failure to indicate at roundabouts or when turning left (or right) and not looking in the mirror while reversing.

Mr Heffernan felt he had been 'blacklisted', saying that none of these so-called errors occurred when he went out with his driving instructor (and friend) Pat O'Mahony.

JACK BLACK

Born to a working-class Irish migrant family in Birkenhead, Jack Black became one of the low-life characters immortalised in Henry Mayhew's famous book *London Labour and the London Poor*.

He became famous during the 1850's as London's top rat-catcher, and distributed handbills proclaiming himself 'Rat and Mole Destroyer to Her Majesty'. He even had his own rat-catching uniform, which consisted of a top hat, a scarlet topcoat worn over a once-yellow silk waistcoat and white leather breeches full of bite marks and holes. His costume was completed with a large black leather sash, inlaid with cast-iron rats.

Whilst down the sewers, if he caught any rats of an interesting colour he would breed from them and try to establish new colour varieties. He would then sell his home-bred rats as pets – mainly, as Black observed, 'to well-bred young ladies to keep in squirrel cages'.

Beatrix Potter, in-between writing about Peter Rabbit and his friends, also found time to buy a rat from him. Obviously impressed, she then dedicated the book *Samuel Whiskers* to her rat of the same name.

The ladies of the court were smitten with this new fashion and they kept their rats in dainty gilded cages. Rumour has it that even Queen Victoria herself kept a rat or two.

A rat-catcher from childhood, Black's main income came from supplying publicans with rats for 'rat matches'. These took place in special pits in which dogs would be matched against each other, and bets would be taken on which would kill the most rats. It was obviously very lucrative, as catchers were paid three pence for each rat caught, and one London landlord had a standing order of 20,000 rats per year.

Rat-catching was not for the faint-hearted, as there was always the danger of infection from the bite of a sewer rat. Black was reported to have said:

> When the bite is a bad one it festers and forms a hard core in the ulcer, which throbs very much indeed. This core is as big as a boiled fish's eye, and as hard as stone. I generally cuts the bite out clean with a lancet and squeezes … I've been bitten nearly everywhere, even where I can't name to you, sir.

MARTIN NEE

During the post-war years, there was always a very real threat of yet another confrontation as the USA and the Soviet Union, the two main Cold War antagonists, dominated international affairs for decades. Much has been written about the period, but there is an interesting footnote to these events on the world stage in the rather bizarre decision made by an Irishman.

On 13 November 1953, a fellow named Martin Nee decided to defect to East Germany. It appears that Nee was serving with the British Army in the western zone of Berlin at the time. Sometime after his defection a statement from the Communist government was released, with the bold Nee reported to have said, 'I want to do everything I can to prevent a third world war, so that is why I have come here.'

Rather frustratingly, there is no record of what became of him.

AMANDA ROS (1860-1939)

A schoolmistress from Larne in County Antrim could arguably be a candidate for the worst novelist in history. The redoubtable Amanda Ros was convinced that she was deserving of a place within the pantheon of literary gods.

The author of the classics *Irene Iddlesleigh* and *Delina Delaney* seemed to be a sensitive soul as she took umbrage at any form of criticism of her finely honed craft.She even went to the extent of having cards printed with 'At Home

Always To The Honourable' – although to her eyes most of the literary world were dishonourable and in particular were the critics, who she termed as 'evil minded earthworms'. She believed that the cause of their hostility towards her was simply because they were in love with her.

In 1889, a Mr Payne wrote in a review of her novel, *Irene Iddlesleigh*, that:

> The book has not amused. It began by doing that. Then, as its enormities went on getting more and more enormous in every line, the book seemed something titanic, gigantic, awe-inspiring. The world was full of *Irene Iddesleigh*, by Mrs. Amanda McKittrick Ros, and I shrank before it in tears and in terror.

So, just how bad was her writing? An excerpt from Irene Iddlesleigh's soliloquy on her wedding night may give you an idea:

> Leave me now deceptive demons of deluded mockery; lurk no more around the vale of vanity, like a vindictive viper, strike the lyre of living deception to the strains of dull deadness, despair and doubt

Her talent for alliterative naming puts the old girl, in her own inimitable way, on a par with Charles Dickens. However, in her unpublished novel, *Helen Huddleston*, she furnishes the cast with names of fruits, such as Lord Raspberry and his sister Cherry, Sir Peter Plum, the Earl of Grape, Sir Christopher Currant, and Lady Pear.

I was particularly taken with her description of 'ladies bits' in this most peculiar passage from the above-mentioned book:

... as those grey eyes looked in bashful tenderness into
the glittering jet revolvers that reflected their sparkling
lustre from nave to circumference, casting a deepened
brightness over the whole features of an innocent girl,
and expressing, in invisible silence, the thoughts, nay,
even the wish, of a fleshy triangle whose base had been
bitten by order of the Bodiless Thinker.

Until the 1930s, when her books were reprinted by Chatto
& Windus, copies were difficult to obtain because Mrs Ros,
distrusting publishers, always printed and published her
own writings.

Her works were in fact much sought after by connoisseurs
of kitsch, and members of the Oxford Amanda Ros Society,
established in 1907, would hold weekly readings of Ros.
This was, naturally, gratifying, but Amanda Ros needed
no one to remind her that she was a genius. She took her
gift very seriously, always signing herself as 'Amanda Ros,
Author'. She even considered putting herself forward for the
Nobel Prize for Literature in 1930, but decided against it
when she discovered that, if she won, she would have to
travel to Oslo instead of them visiting her.

About the same time, The Inklings, an Oxford literary
group that included C.S. Lewis and J.R.R Tolkien, held
competitions to see who could read Ros' work aloud for
the longest length of time without laughing. Her fame even
reached America, where Mark Twain crowned her 'Queen
and Empress of the Hogwash Guild.'

She also wrote poetry and published *Poems of Puncture*
(1932) and *Fumes of Formation* (1933). From the latter
is the opening verse of her Homeric epic 'On Visiting
Westminster Abbey':

Holy Moses! Take a look!
Flesh decayed in every nook
Some rare bits of brain lie here
Mortal loads of beef and beer.

JOHNNY ROCHE

This was a man who decided to build himself a castle in County Cork with nothing more in the way of tools than a spade, a shovel and a rickety old cart.

For three long years, from 1867 to 1870, he sweated and laboured, gathering stones from the river by hand, digging away furiously, and drawing lime in his ancient cart that was pulled by an equally ancient donkey. As the castle grew higher and higher, he invented a winch to draw up the stones. People came from many miles just to stare. They called it 'Castle Curious' and obviously thought that its builder was pretty curious too.

Roche was the son of a carpenter and blacksmith from Wallstown near Mallow, County Cork, who had emigrated to America to make his fortune but returned empty-handed. Back in County Cork he tried running a mill, but when that failed he turned his hand to making tombstones. He was a man of many talents, as he could also draw teeth; indeed he used to make false teeth from cows' hooves. He could also mend clocks, play the bagpipes and the violin, and was an accomplished dancer and singer.

When it was finally finished, the castle comprised an oval tower over 40ft high, topped by two more oval turrets at right angles to the main building, and complete with a drawbridge. At the base of the tower, a slab of granite was engraved with the lettering 'John Roche 1870'. One of the turrets carried a flag with a dying angel and the walls were ornamented with gargoyles. When this peculiar castle with its labyrinth of tiny rooms was complete, Roche confounded the locals, all of whom were convinced he was mad, by moving in and living there for the rest of his life.

Roche was not fond of visitors and he would frequently pull up his drawbridge to discourage them. He was, however, by no means a recluse. He travelled about the countryside on a home-made bicycle or in a ramshackle coach drawn by two donkeys and equipped with a bed and stove.

His best friend, a retired Dragoon called Nixon, was so impressed by his talents that he asked Roche to design his tombstone if he should die first. In due course the master builder erected a flagpole over the grave, with the not particularly imaginative inscription 'HERE LIES NIXON'. He had planned for something far more elaborate for himself, but he died before he could carry his plans out. However, his epitaph survives:

Here lies the body of poor John Roche
He had his faults, but don't reproach
For while alive his heart was mellow
An artist, genius and gentle fellow

JONATHAN SWIFT (1667-1745)

The famous author of *Gulliver's Travels* was originally a churchman who later became the Dean of St Patrick's

Cathedral. His first appointment was as the rector of a small church in County Antrim. Here he started to develop the strange behaviour that would eventually mark him as one of Ireland's most notable eccentrics.

Much like Charles Parnell, he had an obsession with counting. He would frequently tell anyone within earshot the exact number of steps he would take from one location to another.

Doctors now agree that his legendary rudeness to people was probably due to a condition he had that caused gritty matter to build up in his bladder. There was an occasion when, whilst in a coffee shop, a man was writing a letter and asked Swift if he had any sand (the purpose of which was to dry the ink). 'No Sir,' Swift replied, 'but I have the gravel. If you give me your letter I'll piss on it.'

Swift was the ultimate curmudgeon. He disliked nearly everything, but was particularly resentful of women, small children, and anyone from Scotland. In one of his essays, he wrote that women were 'a sort of species hardly a degree above the monkey'. Warming to the subject, he added that no woman was 'worth giving up the middle of your bed for'.

Within his satirical essay 'A Modest Proposal' he suggested a rather novel approach to the Irish over-population problem by suggesting that they eat their babies.

Another of his many obsessions was bodily functions. In 1733 he wrote a book on the subject called Human Ordure, under the pen name Dr Shit. He was also the author of two books about flatulence: *The Benefit of Farting Explained* (1722) and *Ars Musica; or The Lady's Back Report* under the name of Countess of Fizzlerump (1723).

Swift dreaded old age and the senility that would go with it. He once remarked to a friend, 'I shall die like a tree, from the top.' Sadly, he did succumb to a form of dementia and in his more lucid moments became convinced that he could stave it off by a mixture of brisk exercise and specially designed diets. He then got into the habit of eating his meals while walking round the room.

Madness and eccentricity were themes that followed him through his life, and that was confirmed in *Verses on the Death of Dr Swift* (1731),in which he wrote, 'He gave the little wealth he had, To build a house for fools and mad; And show'd by one satiric touch, No nation wanted it so much.' And his 'house for fools and mad' was eventually built, as he had bequeathed from his will the sum of £12,000 to found St Patrick's Hospital, the first of its kind to cater for mental illness in Ireland.

'A VERY ANGRY ENGLISHMAN'

In the eighteenth century an unnamed Englishman. who appeared to have had a pathological hatred of the Irish, inherited a property in County Tipperary, but only on the strict condition that he had to live there. He had no choice but to agree, and he proved to be a very unpopular and disagreeable neighbour. When he died in 1791 his rather eccentric will revealed the following bequest.

Every year on the anniversary of his death, the sum of £8 was to be used to buy a cask of whiskey, and this was to be given to no more than twenty-five Irishmen, who were then to meet in the graveyard in which he was buried. The whiskey was to be poured out into large flagons, and each Irishman was to be given 'a stout oaken stick and a sharp knife'. His will concluded:

Knowing what I know of the Irish character my conviction is that with these materials given, they will not fail to destroy each other and when, in the course of time, the race comes to be exterminated this neighbourhood at least may perhaps be colonised by civilised and respectable Englishmen.

ADOLPHUS COOKE (1792-1876)

Adolphus Cook was perhaps one of the strangest landlords Westmeath – or indeed Ireland – had ever seen. A very wel-read man, he had declared himself a Buddhist and fervently believed in reincarnation. He was convinced that one of the turkeys in the farmyard was his late father, and servants had to doff their hats or curtsey when it waddled by.

Cooke then had all the windows and doors ripped out of his stately home and rebuilt with arches to match a set of curved-back dining chairs he was particularly fond of.

This loopy landowner would lead his workmen out each day, marching at the head of a line of wheelbarrows. In order to keep their jobs, they had to conform to some rather strange rules.

Animals were no exception to this. One day the family dog was put on trial for 'wandering off the estate in a wilful manner'. The dog sat while witnesses from Cooke's workforce gave evidence to a 'jury'. After retiring for a couple of hours, they returned a 'guilty' verdict and the judge passed the death sentence. A quick-thinking servant, who had been appointed hangman, claimed that the dog had spoken to him on the way to the gallows. Cooke, always looking for evidence of reincarnation immediately reprieved him.

When a bullock fell into a pond on his estate and drowned, Cooke had his workers round up all the cattle and march them slowly past the floating corpse as an awful warning of what could happen if they stumbled into water without looking where they put their hooves.

Even though hunting was a major pastime for the wealthy, he refused to take part in it, as he was convinced that he would be reincarnated as a fox. As a result of this, he was in the habit of wandering around the countryside checking for possible exit points for him to escape the hounds.

Perhaps the strangest story about Cooke was the 'affair of the crows'. After being awoken one morning by the noise of crows nesting nearby, he ordered his workmen to collect twigs and branches and build new nests for the crows far away from the house. When he turned up to inspect the work, he wanted to know why they were unoccupied. His workers then explained that 'his' crows had been involved in a bitter feud with the crows of a neighbouring landowner about the new nests, and a huge battle had taken place. Cooke was pleased to hear that his crows were victorious and then asked to see the dead crows. The workmen then told him that the neighbouring crows had called a truce and flew over to collect all the casualties. Cooke was delighted and gave a reward to all of his men.

In-keeping with his general eccentricities, he designed and built his own tomb to look like a beehive, as he was also convinced that he might be reincarnated as a bee – there was even a hole at the tip of the tomb for him to fly out of. He had it fitted with bookcases, chairs and a table, and left instructions that he should be buried sitting upright in front of a fire, which was to be kept lit.

JENNY HODGERS AKA
ALBERT CASHIER (1843-1915)

Born on Christmas Day 1843 in Clogherhead, County Louth, the young Jenny started dressing in men's clothes at a young age. No doubt shunned by her family and neighbours, she left home on her eighteenth birthday to emigrate to the United States.

She arrived just as the Civil War had begun and, using the name of 'Albert Cashier', she then joined the Union Army and proceeded to fight for them for the next three years. By all accounts she seems to have fought in over forty battles, and no one was ever the wiser to the true identity of the small and quiet soldier.

In 1865 Jenny finally left the army and, for the next forty years, lived a quiet and uneventful life in a small town in Illinois. As she was still dressing and living as a man, she obviously continued to keep her army pension.

However everything changed following an accident in 1911, when the 68-year-old was hit by a car and suffered a broken leg. The doctor treating 'Albert' was astonished to discover that she was in fact a woman. And, perhaps out of respect for her service in the military, he decided to keep it a secret.

A few years later, however, Jenny developed dementia and was placed into an asylum, where it quickly became apparent that the old soldier was in fact a woman. Now forced to wear women's clothes for the first time in over fifty years, Jenny found the long dresses difficult to walk in and one day tripped over the hem and broke her hip. While recuperating from this accident, she had also come under investigation from the authorities over her eligibility for a military pension. On hearing of her dilemma, her former comrades wrote a letter stating that she had fought as well as any man in the battlefield and was well-deserving of the pension. Happily, the government body saw sense, backed down and let her keep her pension.

She died a few years later (in trousers) in 1915.

JOHN RUTTER CARDEN (1811-66)

By the time John Rutter Carden took over the estate in Templemore, County Tipperary, following his father's death it had long been neglected, and as the tenants previously had not been paying any rent it appeared highly unlikely that they were about to start now.

Seemingly given no choice in the matter, Carden decided to start evicting families from the estate. This did not go well for Carden, as his tenants then went to great lengths to try and kill him. All their attempts failed, and as a result he came to be known as 'Woodcock Carden'. (It seems that startled woodcocks fly with such erratic and twisting movements that they are almost impossible to shoot.)

But it is for what happened on his forty-first birthday that he is best remembered. He fell hopelessly in love with the 18-year-old Eleanor Arbuthnot who, by coincidence, was also a wealthy heiress. Her family unsurprisingly forbade the much older and deeply unpopular Carden to have anything to do with her. Nevertheless, he was so besotted with her and so determined to have her as his wife that he decided to kidnap her.

He carefully hatched a (not particularly) cunning plan, whereby Eleanor was to be seized while returning home from church. He then organised relay-teams of horses to be posted along the road to Galway where he would take his bride-to-be. The kidnap went spectacularly wrong when his hired help went to the wrong location, his spare horse went lame, and Eleanor's aunt beat off his kidnap attempt by hitting him with an umbrella. Rutter, deprived of his prize and with a bloody nose, jumped back into his carriage and fled. A few hours later he was eventually captured when one of his horses dropped dead on the road to Clonmel.

He was tried four weeks later in Clonmel Courthouse where he was found 'Not Guilty' of abduction, but 'Guilty' of attempted abduction. Carden was then sentenced to two years in jail with hard labour. He was offered a chance to be released if he promised to agree not to 'annoy or molest' Eleanor Arbuthnot. He refused to sign the undertaking and off he went to prison.

Following his release from prison in 1856, you would have thought his ardour would have cooled. This was certainly not the case, as the lovestruck Carden still continued to follow Eleanor all over Ireland.

Carden died in 1866, still unmarried. But it appeared that he was not as bad as he was originally painted, for he had improved the existing houses on the estate, paid decent wages to his workmen and built a school for the children of his tenants. Conversely, Eleanor was now perceived as haughty, arrogant and heartless, and was frequently hissed at when seen out in public. She too never married, and seemed to have lived out the rest of her life away from the public gaze.

PADDY O'CONNELL

In 1840 a Lieutenant Charles Wilkes, on the staff of an American mapping expedition, stepped ashore on one of the islands of Fiji. He was instantly greeted by a red-headed man dressed in the traditional garb of the Islanders who spoke English with an accent he could not quite place. It was in fact a Clare accent, belonging to man called Paddy O'Connell. O'Connell told the somewhat bewildered Wilkes that he had been living in Fiji for over forty years. He then proudly announced that he had fathered forty-eight children and hoped to reach fifty before he died.

SAMUEL BECKETT (1906-89)

When the playwright Samuel Beckett lived briefly in Berlin, one of his favourite places to have lunch was in a small restaurant called The Giraffe. While sitting there one day, gloomily staring out of the window, he was asked by his waiter, 'Why is there no expression of hope in your work?' After a trademark Beckett silence, he picked up a crumb of bread from the tablecloth, stared at it, then replied – paraphrasing Dante – 'I would have written over the Gates of Heaven what is said to be written over Hell – abandon all hope who enter here.' Beckett then dropped the bread crumb and added, 'That's what I think of hope.'

WILLIAM NORMAN

William Norman, who managed both the Blackpool and Huddersfield football teams after the First World War, was the son of Irish parents who moved to England for work in the factories of the area. This ex-sergeant major, with his waxed moustache and harsh training regime, was an imposing figure. He brought with him his experience of military drills and discipline.

His training involved no kicking of balls, just stamina building exercises, which would include sixty circuits of the field. He had no time for softies, as was illustrated on a bitterly cold day when his players were reluctant to strip off their warm everyday clothes for training. Seeing this, Norman promptly removed all of his clothes and rolled around naked in the snow.

CAPTAIN D'ARCY

Few people have been more desperate to win the Grand National than the Irish jockey Captain D'Arcy. He decided to ride his own horse, The Knight of Gwynne, in the renewal of the 1849 race. D'Arcy had backed himself heavily to win – and needed the bet to come in, as he was in a lot of debt.

So imagine his panic when entering the home straight, to find himself trailing the jockey Thomas Cunningham on his horse, Peter Simple, by several lengths and showing no signs of closing the gap. Desperate situations call for desperate measures, and so the not-so-gallant Captain decided to resort to appealing to the basest of human instincts – greed.

All the way to the line, in a bid to secure his bet, D'Arcy shouted out bribes to Cunningham, urging the man to 'take a pull'. The offer started at £1,000, but as the winning post drew ever nearer, D'Arcy had increased it to £4,000. Unhappily for the captain, but not for the good name of racing, Cunningham was an honourable man and ignored the pleas. He and Peter Simple went on to win by three lengths.

History does not recall what happened to the dishonourable Captain.

THE MISSES STEVENSON

Queen's Square College, a fashionable school of etiquette that was founded in London in the early nineteenth century, became known as 'the Ladies' Eton'. It was run by two formidable and eccentric sisters, the Misses Stevensons, who were originally from Dublin. The college was exclusively for the daughters of the growing middle classes. Unfortunately there is very little known about the two sisters except for their lessons in etiquette, which were deemed a vital part of a young lady's education. Some examples on how to behave were:

When dining, never make noises with the mouth or throat. Never permit yourself to use gestures, or illustrations made with a knife or fork on the tablecloth.

Do not speak in conversations if you have nothing of interest to say to someone. Do not discuss the weather.

A gentleman may walk between two ladies, but a lady must never walk between two gentlemen.

No gentleman should use his bare hand to press the waist of a lady in the waltz. If without gloves, he should carry a handkerchief in his hand. Likewise, a lady should not touch a person without gloves on. Ladies are to wear gloves in public places and not take them off to shake hands.

Swinging the arms when walking, eating on the street, sucking parasol handles, pushing roughly through a crowd, talking and laughing very loudly and boisterously on the streets, and whispering in public conveyances are all evidences of ill-breeding.

A lady should not show her legs or even say the word 'leg'. They are properly referred to as 'limbs'

Since the whole point of going to an etiquette school was to marry well, it was important to find the right partner. The Stevenson sisters relied on the 'principles of politeness', which gave the rules for selection:

A tall man could be paired with a shorter woman.

People with eyes of blue, gray, black, or hazel should not marry people with the same eye colour.

People with thin, wiry features and 'cold blood' should marry those with round features and 'warm blood.'

Those with bright red hair and a florid complexion have

an excitable temper and should marry a person with very dark black hair or possibly a brunette.

Soft, fine haired people should not marry people like themselves.

People with curly hair should marry those with straight hair.

Irritable, nervous people should marry sympathetic, quiet types.

Quick-speaking people should marry someone calm and deliberate.

People who do not fit into one specific category (ie not blonde or brunette) or are average (not tall or short) should marry someone similar to themselves.

SEAMUS BURKE (1888-1959)

Kilkenny-born Seamus Burke became famous for being the world's first 'enter-ologist'. This was the opposite of escapology as it involved entering, rather than escaping from, the usual boxes, chains and other devices.

Burke, who never went to school, worked as a labourer around Dublin for a while, before deciding to become a hermit and built a small shack in the Wicklow Mountains, where he lived for a number of years. One day, after reading an article about Houdini, the idea came to him of being an 'enter-ologist'. Burke then headed for England to launch his new career. Within six months he had perfected his act and gave his first show on 16 December 1935 at The New Hippodrome in Manchester.

He was an instant success and was rewarded with a two-year contract to tour the country. His new act involved three different tricks. He would first get into a trunk that had been wrapped with chains and sealed with wax. He would then appear in a large, sealed brown paper bag after he had been tied to a chair. Finally he was strapped to a chair with a knotted bag resting on his knees, and after the screens were removed, he was inside the bag and still strapped to the chair.

After dislocating his shoulder following an unsavoury incident involving the wife of a ventriloquist, a hotel room and a shaving brush, he started to cut back on his shows until he disappeared back into obscurity sometime in the late 1930s.

PETER LANGAN (1941-88)

The wonderfully bonkers restaurateur Peter Langan was the son of the famous Irish rugby fullback Dan Langan. Originally from County Clare, he somehow ended up as the chef at Odin's restaurant in Devonshire Street, Marylebone, where he first started displaying the eccentricities that became his trademark.

In 1976 he opened a new restaurant, Langan's, in Piccadilly, in a seemingly unlikely partnership with the film actor Michael Caine and the chef Richard Shepherd. The restaurant quickly became a well-known haunt for the rich and famous. This was helped by Langan's peculiar behaviour, which kept the restaurant in the public eye.

Stories about him were legendary. One evening a cockroach was found in the ladies toilet. Langan approached the customer, examined the cockroach closely and denied any responsibility. 'Madam,' he said, 'this cockroach is dead. All ours are alive.' He then proceeded to swallow it and washed it down with the customer's glass of champagne.

It did not matter whether you were famous or not, as he treated all his customers the same. For example, there was the time when Princess Margaret and a few friends had just finished their meal and Langan stumbled over, climbed on to the table and promptly fell asleep. He once asked Prince Albert of Monaco 'Is it true you're a f***ing poof?' and he decided to bar Rudolf Nureyev 'for being himself'; he also refused to serve Marlon Brando for being too fat. It appears that diners were only safe from his attentions later in the evening, as he tended to pass out on the floor of the gentleman's lavatory.

In his final years, Langan desperately wanted to franchise his name in America. This he finally achieved in 1986 when Langan's Brasserie opened in New York. Hardly surprisingly, Langan himself was quickly barred from the premises.

Sadly, before he could reap the rewards of his success, he went to sleep one night whilst still smoking a cigarette and set fire to the bed, the house and himself.

RICHARD KIRWAN (1733-1812)

Richard Kirwan, known as 'the Philosopher of Dublin', was perhaps one of the most eccentric men of his time. Kirwan became well-known in the scientific community for his work in the new sciences of meteorology and climatology, and is perhaps the father of the modern weather forecast.

He did, however, have some rather odd beliefs in other matters. He was convinced that he had proved a mysterious element called Philogiston was released by melting certain metals, so he wrote an essay on his new discovery in 1707 to great acclaim. But later that year the French scientist Lavoisier read it and wrote an opposing essay, completely rubbishing the theory and – more to the point – disproving it.

Kirwan was horrified and, with his good name as a scientist in tatters, he completely withdrew from scientific pursuits. He was not, however, put off from advancing similarly odd arguments that he published on a regular basis, some of which included an argument that mankind's first language was Ancient Greek and a study on the efficacy of tobacco smoke enemas.

Kirwan also followed a decidedly odd diet. All he would eat was ham and milk. The ham was cooked on a Sunday, then reheated and served throughout the rest of the week.

He was also was obsessed with not catching a cold. All year round he would keep a blazing fire in his living room, even on the hottest days. One of his theories was that the body could store heat, so he always wore an overcoat and an enormous wide-brimmed hat indoors, to prevent any heat escaping from his head. If he intended to go out, he would stand in front of the fire for at least thirty minutes, in order to absorb as much 'calorific' as possible. When walking he would refuse to acknowledge anybody by speaking, as he insisted on keeping his mouth closed so none of the precious heat could escape. He was once asked why he never attended church; he replied that it would mean having to take his hat off.

Kirwan also had a pet eagle, which he was very fond of. He had trained it so that it would always fly away and land on his shoulder. However, his pet met a grisly end when a well-meaning acquaintance saw the eagle swooping down towards Kirwan and, fearing the bird would attack him, shot it with a pistol.

His domestic life was equally strange, as he shared his home with a long-suffering (but presumably well-paid) manservant called Pope. Poor old Pope had to get up in the middle of the night and pour hot tea down the sleeping Kirwan's throat. Kirwan was adamant that this nocturnal tea drinking was absolutely necessary in order to maintain his correct body temperature through the night.

Another of Kirwan's many eccentricities was a hatred of flies. He would pay Pope a silver coin for every twenty-five flies he brought to him.

In spite of Kirwan's many neuroses, his home was a popular rendezvous for his fellow academics. Every Thursday and Friday he would receive his visitors while lying on his back, wrapped in a rug in front of the constantly roaring fire.

Another of his seemingly endless list of eccentricities was an obsession with time. His soirées had to begin at six o'clock on the dot and finished at exactly nine o'clock. At the stroke of six he would instruct Pope to remove the door knocker to prevent any disruption of the conversations. At nine o'clock, he would suddenly stop talking and point towards the door.

Despite all his precautions over his health, he insisted on trying the then fashionable remedy of starving a cold – with fatal results. Complications set in and he died soon after, at the age of 97.

JOHN JACKSON (1824-1901)

Born in Suffolk to an Irish mother, Jackson played first-class cricket for Nottinghamshire and was a fearsome fast bowler. He was given the nickname 'Foghorn' due to his habit of blowing his nose very loudly after taking a wicket. Over 6ft tall and weighing over 15 stone, Jackson terrorised batsmen.

In 1860 whilst playing against Surrey, he took all ten wickets and sent four batsmen to hospital by hitting them on the head. The last batsman received a particularly hostile delivery that struck him on the foot. He was given not out. 'Maybe not,' the batsman said, 'but I'm going anyway.'

CONSTANTIA PHILLIPS (1702-65)

Born in 1702 after her father Captain Thomas Phillips moved his family to London. The young Constantia seemed perfectly content with her life and started work as a seamstress. Following some kind of Damascene moment in the summer of 1718, she left her job and set herself up as a courtesan. By all accounts she did very well at it and boasted some rather influential people as her clients. After reaching the ripe old age of 30 she decided to retire and with her savings opened The Green Cannister, London's first sex shop, in what is now Bedford Street. It appears that by far the most popular item of merchandise were her 'preservatives' or condoms.

Condoms, or 'cundums' as they were known, had been recorded in popular use since around 1500. In 1740, a Roger Pheuqewll Esq, described the condom his A New Description of Merryland as being 'made of an extraordinary fine thin Substance. And contrived so as to be of one piece and without a Seam, only about the Bottom it is generally bound round with a Scarlet Ribbon for ornament.'

They were made from sheeps intestines and had to be soaked in water to keep them sufficiently pliable for use. Despite these obvious disadvantages, they seemed to be very popular. Casanova swore by them and bought them by the box whenever he found a reliable source. The writer James Boswell became an avid fan, boasting that he invited a comely wench to Westminster Bridge and there 'in armour complete did I enjoy her upon this noble edifice'. But even Boswell was not always satisfied: His diary reports in 1764, 'Quite agitated. Put on condom; entered. Heart beat; fell. Quite sorry ...'.

Incidentally, the name 'cundum' first appeared in English in 1665, in a poem, 'A Panegyric upon Cundum', by the syphilitic literary genius John Wilmot, the Earl of Rochester. For many years, it was rumoured that a certain Colonel Condom, the Royal Physician, had invented the device for the randy King Charles II to stop him producing more bastard progeny, but it has now been found that he never existed.)

The remarkable Mrs Phillips appears to have been well stocked, as flyers of the time show advertisments for 'Widow's comforters' in leather, ivory and wood. She also supplied Flagellation machines for the 'discerning gentleman' and offered pamphlets on the 'education of young ladies'.

Even though Mrs Phillips appeared to do a roaring trade, The Green Canister did not make her fortune. She had several marriages and even more affairs, and eventually left England for Jamaica, where she died of a fever in 1765.

COLONEL WILLIAM HALL-WALKER (1856-1933)

In 1900, Colonel William Hall-Walker, founded the Irish National Stud Farm.

The colonel was a great believer in astrology and also appears to have been an early devotee of Feng Shui, as all the buildings were designed and placed in such a way to provide the best possible astrological influences on the occupants. He would carefully note the exact birth time of each of his foals and his own astrologer, imported at great expense from India, would draw up their astrological charts. The foals with promising indicators he kept and raced. Those with bad charts he sold immediately, regardless of breeding or confirmation.

The horses he bred that then went on to win races further convinced him that it was all due to favourable astrological influences. An extremely bad-tempered man, he would often sack any of his trainers whose horses did not live up to their destinies.

Hall-Walker's copy of the horoscopes for his 1911 foals contain some wonderfully wacky predictions. One in particular was about a horse called Carrickfergus. He wrote: 'Hopeless ... you might as well take his shoes off and let him run loose in the paddock.' It was a good job that his trainer did not listen to him, as the following year he went through the season unbeaten and also won the St James's Palace Stakes at Ascot.

MARY MCMULLEN

During the early nineteenth century there were a number of short-lived crazes, one of which was long-distance walking – walking for money.

One of the most successful long-distance walkers was an Irishwoman called Mary McMullen. She became known as 'The Female Pedestrian'. She was described as a thin and tall woman who wore a long dark dress, a coloured scarf and a white muslin cap. The eccentric Mrs McMullen also preferred to walk in bare feet. She could travel 20 miles inside four hours, 40 miles inside nine, and 92 miles within a day. In search of the prize money on offer, she would walk in front of large crowds; one particular event drew over 7,000 spectators.

Over a two-month period sometime in 1826, she completed six long-distance walks – three of 92 miles, one of 40 miles and two of 20. And the truly remarkable thing was that she was well into her 60s at this time.

ABRAHAM ABELL (1773-1851)

Abraham Abell from Cork was an antiquarian, a successful businessman and also a philanthropist. He did, however, have some rather endearing and eccentric habits.

He enjoyed reading so much that he would often read late into the night and, anxious not to fall asleep, he would read standing up. He also refused to have a fire in his room because of the possible danger to his many books. Instead, in order to keep warm, he would take a few turns with a skipping rope.

He also had a most peculiar morning ritual, whereby he would stand on a stool and, with the use of a silk handkerchief, charge himself up with enough static electricity to get him through the day.

There was also the occasion when, after reading a number of ghost stories, he started to get nightmares. He remedied this by buying a skeleton and sleeping with it for a week until the nightmares ceased.

When he died in February 1851 he left behind nearly 5,000 books, his collection of ancient relics and coins ... and his skipping rope.

CAPTAIN DANIEL MALCOM (1725-69)

Malcom was a successful sea captain and part-time smuggler who was greatly opposed the recently introduced Revenue Acts. There was a rising groundswell of opinion that these new Revenue Acts were nothing more than 'taxation without representation'. Increasingly annoyed over these taxes, Malcom decided that enough was enough. A few months after the taxes were introduced, he decided that he would not pay any duty on a consignment of wines that he had just brought in. So one evening, under the cover of darkness, he arranged for the eighty casks of wine he had aboard his ship to be brought ashore. To avoid prying eyes, he dressed the barrels up in women's bonnets and clothes. Once upon dry land the dressed-up barrels were dispersed around the town. Shortly afterwards a meeting was held by the other merchants in the town, and it was agreed that no English goods, other than those used in the fishing industry, would be purchased from England for eighteen months, which, unbeknownst to them, unwittingly sowed the seeds for the forthcoming War of Independence.

Malcom died just before the Battle of Bunker Hill in 1769 and asked to be buried 'in a stone grave 10 feet deep' to be safe from British bullets. Defiant to the end, his opposition to the British taxation policies were carved on his headstone in the Copps Burial Ground in North Boston.

Here he's buried in a
Stone Grave 10 feet deep
Cap DANIEL MALCOLM Mercht
who departed this Life
october 23rd 1769
Aged 44 Years
a true son of Liberty
a Friend to the Publick
An Enemy to oppression
and one of the foremost
in opposing the Revenue Acts
on America.

You can still see the bullet holes from the bullets fired by British soldiers who sought out his grave and used it for target practice.

'AN OLD GENTLEWOMAN'

In one of his letters to a friend, Jonathan Swift described a wonderfully strange occurrence that had recently taken place in Dublin:

> An old gentlewoman died here [in Dublin] two months ago and left in her will instructions that eight men and eight maids should act as coffin bearers and will be paid two guineas each, a further 10 guineas will go to the Parson for the sermon, and two guineas for the clerk. But bearers, parson and clerk must all be true virgins, and not admitted till they took their oaths of virginity.

Sadly, there is no record of what actually happened, leaving one with the rather unsettling image of the poor woman perhaps still lying unburied.

WILLIAM MONSELL, LORD EMLY OF TERVOE (1812-94)

William Monsell, Lord Emly of Tervoe, was one of the most significant, but now seemingly forgotten, political figures of nineteenth-century Ireland. He was at one point the most prominent lay Catholic in Ireland and the chief spokesman for The Catholic Unionists, a large and influential political group. He was also a reforming landlord and was friends with William Gladstone and Pope Pius IX.

Something must have disagreed with him in the spring of 1879 when, for some reason, he just took to his bed. Doctors came and examined him but there appeared to be nothing physically wrong. Nevertheless, he decided to spend the remaining fifteen years of his life in his bedroom, tucked up in his four-poster bed with the curtains drawn.

FATHER SEAN BREEN (1937-2009)

Known as 'The Racing Priest', Father Sean Breen was a regular fixture at the Cheltenham Festival. Originally from Cavan, he also became well-known for blessing race meetings.

Until 1964 the fun-loving Catholic bishops had forbidden priests from attending horse racing. 'The bishops thought it was wrong and evil for people to go racing, so they banned the priests from going,' recalled Breen, who was one of the first to take advantage when that particular 'Thou shalt not' was relaxed.

Within Father Breen's parish in County Kildare were Punchestown and Naas racecourses. Punchestown has a small embankment just opposite one of the fences and this became known as Priests' Hill. It was from here that the priests would watch the racing without physically attending the meeting, thereby avoiding any form of penance.

In 2005, Breen performed a mass for some 2,000 racegoers at the Thistle Hotel in Cheltenham, and the message in his sermon was 'to pray for winners because they are so hard to get and to pray for Irish winners, no matter what part of the country they come from'.

Hardly surprisingly, Breen faced plenty of criticism over the years for his racing and betting connections, but pointed out, 'There's nothing in the Bible that says you can't gamble. We have to lighten up a bit.' When he did have a bet, his wagers were always modest – no more than a tenner at a time – and he was always a moderate drinker.

Over the forty years he spent at each Cheltenham Festival, he made an effort to catch up with old friends. He once remarked 'Cheltenham is like a checklist, if people aren't there, they are either ill or they're dead.'

His analysis of the form book sometimes extended to other areas. In 2005 he recommended to his friends that Cardinal Ratzinger was a sure fire bet to be the next Pope. 'A few of the lads got on at 13-2, but I did not back him myself out of reverence.'

In-between looking after the spiritual wellbeing of his parishioners, he was also a member of Horse Racing Ireland's bookmaker committee. He became a non-runner in any future festival when he died in 2009.

THE PIG-FACED LADY

In September 1814, residents of Dublin and London were electrified by rumours of a young woman with a human body and the head of a pig, who was supposedly living somewhere in Manchester Square in the west end of London.

According to the story, the lady was from Dublin but, after inheriting a very substantial sum, had come to London in search of a husband with whom to share it. Unfortunately, her plans for marital bliss had gone awry due to her unusual appearance and her inability to speak. She was said to communicate in grunts and would eat her meals only from a silver trough. Within a few months, and fuelled by the popular press, the rumours had been elevated to the status of fact. A number of young men placed advertisements in the papers expressing their desire to meet London's most eligible lady and their suitability for the role of husband.

On 16 February 1815, following a letter to *The Times* from a young man asking them to publish an offer of marriage to the lady in question, the paper carried a wonderfully ascerbic editorial:

There is at present a report, in London, of an Irish woman with a strangely deformed face, resembling that of a pig, who is possessed of a large fortune and we suppose wants all the comforts and conveniences incident to her sex and station. We ourselves unwittingly put in an advertisement from a young woman, offering herself to be her companion; and yesterday morning, a fellow (with a calf's head, we suppose) transmitted to us another advertisement, attended by a one pound note, offering himself to be her husband. We have put his offer in the fire, and shall send his money to some charity, thinking it a pity that such a fool should have any. Our rural friends hardly know what idiots London contains ...

Despite such condemnation, newspapers in Dublin and London continued to publish reports about the Pig-Faced Lady of Manchester Square for several more months, until interest began to wane.

Of the Pig-Faced Lady's fate very little is known, but there was a lovely rumour that she eventually did find an admirer and returned to Ireland with him.

WILLIAM ROWAN HAMILTON (1805-65)

The extraordinary William Rowan Hamilton, who became known as the Irish Einstein, was born in Dominick Street in Dublin in 1805. From an early age it became obvious that he had a keen intellect, as he was speaking five languages before his 7th birthday. His parents anxious to make the most of his potential, despatched him to his uncle – a retired clergyman in Trim.

His uncle believed that In order to make the best use of the day, an early start was essential. This was achieved by a piece of string tied to the young Hamilton's toe which through a hole in the wall the uncle was able to tug in order to rouse the young boy to start his studies.

Whether or not it was due to this peculiar early morning ritual, Hamilton flourished intellectually and not only was one of the youngest graduates ever at Trinity College but completely eclipsed his contemporaries by achieving the highest form of pass in both classics and mathematics. Quickly realising that he had very little aptitude for anything outside academia, he decided to take up the position as the new professor of astronomy, which also gave him scope to research his own ideas in mathematics.

His most famous discovery is of Quaternions (apparently they are non-commutative extensions of complex numbers – whatever they are). It happened one morning on 16 October 1843 when he was lost in thought as he walked along the Royal Canal. He had a 'eureka' moment about the Quaternions, and as he had no notebook to hand he carved the formula into the stone of Brougham Bridge, where it can still be seen today.

He was the stereotypical absent-minded academic, often turning up for lectures at the wrong time or on the wrong day. He never used notes and frequently started a lecture on one subject and would then change tack and start talking about something else entirely, frequently baffling his students.

One of his colleagues reported in his diary that when Hamilton was at his desk working, every surface in his study was covered in papers, with some piles nearly reaching the ceiling. He refused to have the room cleaned and he would frequently bring students in to admire new spider webs.

He also seemed to have alternative views on maintaining health. When going for a walk on a wet day he would insist on rolling himself in the first pool of water he came upon, 'in order that he might be beforehand in the rain'.

The death of his sister and his being trapped in an unhappy marriage were probably both factors in him taking to the demon drink, and he died in 1865 from a severe bout of gout.

JOE MCNAMARA

Picture the scene: a crisp autumn morning on 29 September 2010, suddenly interrupted by the rumble of a cement mixer – emblazoned with the words 'Toxic Bank Anglo' – crashing into the gates of the Irish parliament.

This was the start of Mayo man Joe McNamara's many protests against the way banks were being run, and in particular the ill-fated Anglo Irish Bank.

Two months later, the self-styled 'Anglo Avenger' Joe McNamara was back in Dublin city centre, this time staging a protest from atop a cherry picker crane. When he was later acquitted of criminal damage, he became a popular hero.

In 2012, he took his protest to another level by building his own version of Stonehenge on a hilltop on Achill Island, off the Mayo coast. The 15ft-high circle is 30m in diameter and almost 100m in circumference, with thirty-nine standing stones and lintels. Unfortunately for the Achill Stonehenger, he did not have planning permission and the mean-spirited souls of Mayo County Council sought an injunction for him to pull it all down. Apparently it took more than six months in planning, and it was built during the course of a single weekend.

You would have thought by now he would be satisfied that he had made his point. But no, our plucky avenger appeared in the news again – this time in London. On the morning of Saturday 5 May 2015, Joe McNamara unveiled a 30ft-high sword structure on the banks of the Thames beside Tower Bridge and right in front of the offices of the then Mayor of London, Boris Johnson. The structure consisted of a sword with the letters 'pol' written on it, which was being driven through a heart-shaped Union Jack. A friend of the controversial developer said that the 'pol' is short for 'politicians' and the meaning of structure is that politicians are a sword through the heart of Britain.

A friend remarked, 'Joe was amazed that he was able to carry on on Saturday morning without any objection, right in the middle of London, yet when he did likewise in Achill [with Achillhenge], Mayo County Council were straight down on him'.

CAPTAIN 'GLASS'

During the 'golden age' of sailing ships, the many years spent at sea led some seamen to develop some rather strange eccentricities. One of these was a retired Captain who lived near Quilty, County Clare. He was perfectly sane and rational — apart from the fact that he was convinced that he was made of glass. When he moved around, the captain tied padded cushions around himself to act as protection. On his walks around Quilty he resembled an early incarnation of the Michelin man.

The story goes that one early morning he was awoken suddenly by the sound of his front gate being opened. Curious as to who this visitor could be, he jumped out of bed sans cushions, rushed to the top of the stairs, tripped and fell. 'Broken, by God!' were reported to be his last words, as he lay dying at the foot of the stairs.

PHILLIP CRAMPTON (1777-1858)

Born in Dublin, Crampton was the son of a successful dentist. After university, he joined the army and became a surgeon. When he left the army he was appointed surgeon to the Meath Hospital, and then a few years later he set up the first teaching children's hospital in Ireland or Great Britain. He seemed to have lived an exemplary life, a good example of an eminently sensible man. But he did have one particular foible: murophobia — a fear of rats. He was convinced that his body would be eaten by rats when he died, and so, according to the terms of his will, he was to be buried standing up, encased in concrete.

JAMES SALTER

An Irishman by the name of James Salter was responsible for London's first public museum, which opened in a coffee house near Chelsea Old Church, in 1695. It was originally a barber's shop whose proprietor, James Salter, settled in Chelsea about 1673, having 'come thither from Rodman on the Irish main'.

Salter – or 'Don Saltero', as he later became known – had once been employed as travelling valet to Sir Hans Sloane, whose collection formed the basis of the British Museum. Sloane began to donate unwanted objects to Salter, who took them to his place of business, displayed them in cabinets around the walls and began inviting the public to come in and see them. As word about the collection spread, the barber's shop evolved into Don Saltero's Coffee House and Curiosity Museum. He promoted it as a place of marvels and wonder, as an advertisement placed in *Mist's Weekly Journal* in 1728 shows:

> Monsters of all sorts here are seen,
> Strange things in Nature as they grew so,
> Some relics of the Sheba Queen,
> And fragments of the famed Bob Crusoe.
> Knick-knacks, too, dangle round the wall,
> Some in glass-cases, some on shelf,
> But what's the rarest sight of all?
> YOUR HUMBLE SERVANT SHOWS HIMSELF.

Among the exhibits were: a giant's tooth, a curious piece of metal found in the ruins of Troy, the Pope's infallible candle, manna from Canaan, a necklace made of Job's tears, a leprechaun's foreskin(!) and a sandal that belonged to Pontius Pilate's wife. There was no charge to see the museum, but visitors were expected to buy a cup of coffee or a catalogue for twopence. Poor old Salter was evidently not a good businessman: after a few years he declared bankruptcy and the museum closed. The entire contents were auctioned off in 1799.

BENJAMIN O'NEALE STRATFORD, 6TH EARL OF ALDBOROUGH (1808-75)

Benjamin O'Neale Stratford was the 6th and last Earl of Aldborough and eccentricity seems to have been in the family genes.

His great-grandfather John Stratford, the first Earl, convinced himself that he was descended from William the Conqueror. When it was pointed out that in fact he was not at all related, he took matters into his own hands and created a totally fictitious family tree proving it. This took many years and nearly bankrupted him. In 1775 he displayed his new family arms for the first time. They were authentic, but the problem was that they did not belong to him; they were actually the coat of arms for Alexander the Great. He never had the chance to properly show them off as he died shortly afterwards.

The second Earl was the extravagant Edward Augustus Stratford. He had a mania for building. He built Aldborough

House in Dublin; a model town called Stratford-on-Slaney in County Wicklow; and also made extensive improvements to Belan, the great house built by his father in County Kildare. Edward was also famous for throwing lavish house parties in Belan. His death in 1801 interrupted a rather strange dinner party in which the Earl had invited a hundred young people with the intention of marrying them off to one another. To his family's dismay and no doubt his lawyer's delight, he left over sixty different wills.

The third Earl, John, was a much less welcoming type. He was looked after by a vivacious daughter who, unlike the Earl, loved having people around her and invited guests down by the score. Lord Aldborough would grumpily greet each of his guests with, 'When do you leave? The coach passes Bolton Hill every morning, and I can send you there tomorrow.' He was also known to get up at dawn and shuffle round the garden with a huge basket, picking all the best fruit so that his guests would not have any.

Benjamin O'Neale Stratford, the sixth Earl, was perhaps the dottiest of them all. He had devoted his entire life to building the world's biggest balloon. In the 1830s he constructed a giant hangar on his estate in Stratford Lodge, 40 miles from Dublin, spending the next twenty years working there in total secrecy. He was so fearful of rivals that he kept only one servant. The paranoid Stafford wouldn't even employ a cook, having all his meals cooked in Dublin and delivered daily by mail coach.

The Earl's plan was to fly from Ireland to England and then on across the Channel to France, where he had purchased a plot of land on the banks of the Seine for a landing ground. When war broke out our intrepid hero decided to extend his voyage and contribute to the war effort by flying across Europe, dropping bombs on Russian officers. Unfortunately for his dreams of glory, the war came to an end before the balloon was ready.

One Sunday morning in 1856, tragedy struck when Stratford Lodge went up in flames. Lord Aldborough, who was much less interested in the fate of his historic family home than saving his precious balloon, ran around the blazing estate urging onlookers, 'Save the balloon house, save the balloon!' Although hundreds of buckets of water were flung over the great hanger, the silk balloon was damaged beyond repair.

The Earl was a broken man and lived for a time in the burnt-out hangar, but eventually moved to a hotel in Alicante, Spain. Here he would stay recluse-like in his room, rarely venturing out and would have all his meals sent up by room service. For some reason he would never allow the dirty dishes and cutlery to be collected. His solution to this was quite simple: when one room filled up with dishes and plates, he would simply move to another room and the process would start again. He eventually died in his hotel room surrounded by stacks of dirty dishes in the summer of 1875.

Oddly enough, that was not quite the end of his balloon, as for many years all the fishing rods in the neighbourhood were made out of the pieces of cane salvaged from the wreckage.

CHARLES PARNELL (1846-91)

There is a game popular amongst our young, a mystical formula designed to placate the gods usually in the form of 'If I can hold my breath until the fifth lamppost I will get an X-Box for Christmas.' Charles Parnell, the great Irish politician and nationalist, was particular fond of this game.

Whilst walking home one day with a colleague, he reached the door of his house, only to walk away again. A second approach was made and again he walked away. On being asked what he was doing, Parnell explained that he always kept a mental count of the number of paces required to walk between any two points and could never bring himself to finish a journey if the total contained a number four or a number eight.

Parnell considered both numbers to have a sinister significance for him. Seven he thought a good number, while 'Nine is a real symbol of good luck and I can go in rejoicing.'

The next time you pass the statue of Charles Parnell, at the junction of Parnell Street and O'Connell Street, take a second look. The statue shows another of Parnell's curious habits, that of wearing two overcoats at the same time.

LORD WALLSCOURT (1797-1849)

Lord Wallscourt was a most interesting fellow. A man ahead of his time, he was a pioneering socialist who was much taken with the concept of co-operative communes. After a visit to the co-operative commune at Ralahine, County Clare, he returned to his own estate in Ardfry, County Galway, and immediately set aside 100 acres for his own social experiment. Unlike his contemporaries he also embarked on other philanthropic enterprises, establishing a national school and an agricultural school.

A kind man, he was always looking to improve the living conditions of his tenants. One summer he decided to build a two-storey slate-roofed house as a potential prototype to later replace all the thatched cottages of the area. Unfortunately, it proved just about impossible to find anyone wanting to move into the new property, with tenants explaining that 'it would be mighty cold, and you will be expecting to keep it too clean.' Eventually after standing empty for nearly five years, a newly-wed couple took the place, on the grounds that it was 'better than nothing at all'.

Alas, it is not for his socialist principles he is to be lauded for but his naturist tendencies. After reading a pamphlet on naturism on a visit to London in 1845, he became convinced that the only way to achieve constant good health was to be naked between the hours of 10 a.m. and 4 p.m. This he practised daily. His long-suffering wife insisted that he wore a cowbell around his neck in order to warn the servants of his approach.

It seems that the intended benefits of nakedness did not work, as he died of pneumonia a few years later in 1849.

JOHN PHILPOTT CURRAN (1750-1817)

Born with a speech impediment, John Philpott Curran of Cork went on to be one of the most sought-after lawyers of the day. Educated at Trinity College, he was described as 'the wildest, wittiest and dreamiest of students'. His first trial ended in a farce, though; on being asked to sum up for the judge, he took fright and ran out of the courtroom.

'Stuttering Jack' as he came to be known,was a man of strong principles. There are a number of stories of him preferring to take part in duels rather than compromise his beliefs. He is known to have fought at least five.

A liberal Protestant, he became a champion of the popular Irish causes of the time and defended Wolfe Tone and Napper Tandy in treason cases in the 1790s, which reinforced his popularity

A famously witty man, some of his barbed comments are still in use today, such as, 'His smile is like the silver plate on a coffin,' and 'When I can't talk sense, I talk metaphor.'

There was also the occasion when he was having dinner with the notorious 'hanging judge' John Toler (pages 49–50):

Toler: Curran, is that hung-beef?
Curran: Do try it, my lord, then it is sure to be!

He was once asked by a friend of his, a wealthy tobacconist, to come up with a Latin motto for his new coach. After some thought, he suggested *Quid Rides*. A quid was a lump of chewing tobacco and also slang for a one pound (sterling) and 'rides' is Irish slang for 'shagging'; If you read it purely in Latin, *Quid Rides* translates as 'having a laugh'. Considering that it is a 200-year-old joke, it is still rather funny.

Since he was a young man Curran had always been obsessed with punctuality, and with this in mind he invented a rather odd alarm clock. In a letter to one of his friends he excitedly describes his new invention:

I have contrived a machine in the manner of an hourglass, which awakes me regularly at half past four. Above my head I have suspended two vessels of tin, one above the other. When I go to bed, which is always at ten, I pour a bottle of water into the upper vessel, in the bottom of which is a hole of such a size as to let the water through as to make the lower vessel overflow in six hours and a half.

JOHN JAMES HAMILTON, MARQUIS OF ABERCORN (1756-1818)

This overbearing, rank-conscious Irish peer was so aristocratic that apparently even the king was afraid to talk to him. His servants had to wear white gloves at all times, even in the kitchen, whilst his footmen had to dip their hands in a bowl of rosewater before passing him a plate.

Even in the trying circumstances of his marriage breaking down, Abercorn was anxious that proper standards should be maintained. When he discovered that his second wife was going to leave him for her new lover, he requested that she should leave in the family carriage, so that it could never be said that Lady Abercorn left her husband's roof in a hack chaise.

Abercorn maintained a style of living that was lavish even by the spendthrift standards of the age. One evening, on his way to visit Abercorn, his doctor met a procession of five carriages, twenty outriders and a man on horseback wearing the blue ribbon of the Knights of the Garter. It turned out to be Abercorn himself, on his way back from dining alone at a tavern in a nearby village.

The socially-phobic also Abercorn had a novel approach to his house guests. Visitors to his home were generously accorded the run of the house and were free to do as they wished except for one thing – under no circumstances whatsoever were they permitted to speak to Abercorn himself.

NICHOLAS JOSEPH CALLAN (1799-1864)

Nicholas Callan from Darver, County Louth, was an Irish priest and scientist who, although his name has been somewhat forgotten by historians, was a pioneer of electrical science. He invented the induction coil, a forerunner of the transformer.

Whilst testing his experimental coils, he discovered that there was no mechanism available to measure the strength of the voltage. Always renowned for his resourcefulness, he decided to test his new coils on 'volunteer' seminarians – one of whom was the future Archbishop of Dublin, William Walsh, whom he managed to hospitalise. The college authorities were quite natuarally horrified and forbade him any more experiments on clergymen. Callan then proceeded to electrocute chickens instead.

Always anxious to prove the efficacy of his inventions, he famously arranged a tug of war between a group of students and his electromagnet. It appeared that the students were winning – until he switched the magnet off and they all fell in a heap on the floor, much to his delight.

A few years later in 1841 he unveiled another even larger induction machine, which generated 15in sparks, an estimated 60,000 volts, the largest artificial bolt of electricity of the time.

He was a remarkable man, not just in the field of science. He gave away half of his professor's salary to help the poor. In the words of his obituary: 'His extraordinary piety, his perfect simplicity and unaffected candour endeared him to everyone who knew him.'

GEORGE BERNARD SHAW
(1856-1950)

The Dublin-born playwright was a man of many talents and beliefs. A socialist, vegetarian, and a feminist, he also believed himself to be Shakespeare reincarnated. He wrote over fifty plays, and his most celebrated play, *Pygmalion*, was made into the musical *My Fair Lady*, earning him the double distinction of an Academy Award and a Nobel Prize. Not content with that, he also wrote five novels, many essays and was an accomplished orator.

Shaw claimed that he had sex for the first time at the age of 29 with an Irish widow he met on a train, and rumour has it that they consummated their tryst in their carriage. When he did decide to get married at the age of 42, he discovered on the honeymoon that his wife did not care for sex.

In-between chasing the ladies and writing his plays, he still found time to pose naked in Rodin's *The Thinker* pose and to co-found the London School of Economics.

A fervent vegetarian from an early age, he was once asked to justify this. He replied 'Think of the fierce energy concentrated in an acorn! You bury it in the ground and it explodes into a giant oak! Bury a sheep and nothing happens but decay.'

He once told Michael Collins' grieving sister that Collins was lucky 'that he did not die in a snuffy bed of a trumpery cough'.

He also championed some wonderfully odd causes, one of which was spelling reform. He argued that GHOTI was the way you should spell FISH: the 'gh' sound from 'enough,' the 'o' sound from 'women' and the 'ti' sound from 'action. Try it, it actually makes sense!

In 1935, along with his friend H.G. Wells (who incidentally had some equally peculiar notions of his own) he founded The Smell Society. This was a group dedicated to the elimination of unpleasant smells on the London Underground. Their activities involved handing out sheets of paper impregnated with 'smells of the seaside' to commuters.

Shaw was renowned for his vitality, and was working right up to his death in 1950 when, at the age of 94, he fell off a ladder whilst trying to prune a tree and died with his sister at his side. His last words were, 'Sister, you're trying to keep me alive as an old curiosity. But I am done, I am finished, I am going to die.'

FREDERICK CALVERT (1731-71)

The extremely fat and libidinous eighteenth-century Irishman Frederick Calvert, originally from Baltimore Manor, County Longford, spent most of his life travelling around the many brothels of Europe.

On visiting Turkey, he was so taken with the local customs that he decided to adopt a few for himself. With the help of a local procuress, he recruited a small harem which he took with him whenever he travelled. This flamboyant lifestyle occasionally presented difficulties. When he arrived in Salzburg, accompanied by two eunuchs and nine women, the local police asked him to indicate which one was his wife. Calvert replied that he was not in the habit of discussing his personal arrangements and offered to settle the matter with his fists.

Calvert never returned to Ireland. He remained on the continent, 'constantly moving ... that he might not know where he should be buried'. It was in Naples in September 1771, that after a night with a couple of 'aged' prostitutes, he contracted a fever and died.

COLONEL THOMAS BLOOD (1618-80)

Not Not strictly an eccentric, perhaps more of a rogue, the mysterious Colonel still deserves a mention. He was born in County Clare to a reasonably well-to-do family and on the outbreak of the English Civil War in 1642, he decided to go to England and fight for the Royalists. When it became obvious that Cromwell and his Roundheads were going to win, he quickly changed sides.

He seemed to have done well out of the war (despite initially picking the wrong side), as he somehow talked his way into being given an appointment as a Justice of the Peace. Now this is where things start to get interesting. For some reason, probably money or the lack of it, he got involved in a plot to seize Dublin Castle and take the governor, Lord Ormonde, prisoner. This went spectacularly wrong and he had to flee to Holland. Blood returned in 1670 and decided to set his sights higher – he was going to steal the Crown Jewels.

On the morning of the 15 March 1671 Colonel Blood, accompanied by three friends and dressed as a parson, visited the Tower Of London, where he called the guard over who was looking after the Crown jewels and asked him if he wished to be blessed. And bless him he did, producing a mallet from the folds of his cassock and promptly knocked him out. With the guard out of the way, they picked up the jewels, only to discover that they were too big to hide under their clothing. After wasting valuable time trying to file the Imperial Sceptre in half, they gave up and made off with only the orb and ceremonial crown. They had got no further than the main gate when a huge hue and cry ensued and they were arrested.

Thereafter rumour took over. The punishment for stealing the Crown jewels would normally be lots of torture and death. This did not happen; in fact, Blood and his companions received a free pardon from the king, and Blood himself was rewarded with a position at court. Some scholars now believe that Charles II, who was always short of money, had organised the robbery himself, whilst others are of the opinion that he had a fondness for audacious scoundrels such as Blood and that he was amused by his claim that the jewels were worth only £5,000 as opposed to the £100,000 at which the Crown had valued them. It then came as no surprise when Blood was further rewarded with the deeds to rich tracts of land in Ireland.

When Charles died in 1685, officials were shocked to discover that jewels were missing from the coronation crown and had been replaced by cheap imitations, again adding credence to the theory that the robbery had taken place with Charles's blessing.

There is an amusing epitaph to all of this. When Blood finally died in 1680, his body was exhumed by the authorities for confirmation; such was his reputation for trickery, it was suspected he might have faked his death and funeral to avoid marrying a particularly persistent widow.

BRIAN DE BREFFNY (1931-89)

A man of many names and titles, he was known as Baron O'Rourke de Breffny, sometimes the 7th Baron of the Holy Roman Empire, or simply Count O'Rourke. Whatever he liked to be called, it was in keeping with the large and palatial mansion he kept in Carrick-on Suir-which was staffed with Indian servants.

He was in fact a fake, albeit a very successful one. He was born in Isleworth, Middlesex, the only son of a taxi driver called Maurice Lees. As a young man Lees/de Breffny lived in Rome and worked as a professional genealogist. His interest in the subject had been stimulated when he discovered that his grandmother's name was Breffny. From this he inferred that she must have been related to the Irish O'Rourkes, the Princes of Breffny.

The promiscuous de Breffny married twice, first to an Indian princess, and secondly to a widowed Finn. With a more than generous divorce settlement from his first wife, he moved into the stately Castledown Cox in Kilkenny.

De Breffny did have a serious side. His *Houses of Ireland* (1984) is now considered one of the most authoritative books on the subject. At a time when most of the country was indifferent, even slightly vindictive, about the destruction of these landmarks of the colonial era, de Breffny poured himself into protecting these wonderful buildings.

When he was writing his book, de Breffny used to turn up unannounced and just let himself in. He would then wander around taking notes. Most owners did not seem to mind ,once they found out that he was not in fact a burglar – although on one occasion, when he was in country house in Munster, the lady of the house saw him examining a painting. Thinking that he was up to no good, she grabbed an ancient hunting rifle off the wall and threatened to shoot him if he did not leave. Running down the drive, he bumped into the owner returning on a horse. The flustered de Breffny then berated him on the rudeness of his servants and told him that he would never go there again.

Having reinvented himself in Ireland, de Breffny lived the life of an eccentric millionaire. His wives, and even some of his friends, knew of his real background, but it was only after his death that the full truth was revealed.

ENDYMION

Endymion was the nickname of James Farrell, a well-known Dublin character. Legend has it that whilst working as an excise officer he fell into a vat of gin trying to rescue a colleague. It might not be true, but it still makes for a good story.

Whatever the truth, he became known for his eccentric behaviour. Oliver St John Gogarty describes the flamboyantly dressed Farrell in the opening chapter of his book, *As I Was Going Down Sackville Street*:

> He wore a tailcoat over white cricket trousers, which were caught in at the ankles by a pair of cuffs. A cuff-like collar sloped upwards to keep erect a little sandy head, crowned by a black bowler some sizes too small.'

A creature of habit, every day he would visit the National Library to read all the newspapers. He would then follow a most peculiar ritual when he was leaving. On stepping out of the doors of the library he would march out into the middle of the road, pull a big brass compass from his pocket and, after looking up at the sky for a few minutes, examine the compass and then swiftly march off holding his compass in front of him. He would then come to a stop at the Ballast Office clock, and would gaze at it for a while before pulling out his sword and ceremoniously saluting the clock. His final act would be to produce an enormous alarm clock from his bag and carefully set it to the time on the Ballast Office clock, before returning it to the bag – where it would immediately start ringing loudly as he walked off once again.

THOMAS DOGGETT (1640-1721)

According to the Guinness Book of Records, The Doggetts Coat and Badge Race is the longest-running sporting contest in the world. It was started in 1715 by the Dublin-born actor Thomas Doggett who at the time was the manger of the Drury Lane Theatre. Doggett himself was also a well-known comic actor; his most famous role, as most accounts seem obliged to point out, was as a character named Deputy Nincompoop.

Living on the 'wrong' side of the Thames, Doggett relied on the ferrymen to convey him across the river, and some time in 1715 he fell overboard and had to be rescued. In gratitude he offered a prize for the fastest rower in a single scull between London Bridge and Chelsea – a coat and a badge – and for the last 300 years watermen have been competing for that honour.

Doggett also left a small annuity to pay for a engraved silver medallion (the size of a dinner plate) and instructions that this wonderfully anachronistic race was to be held 'forever'.

FREDERICK HERVEY (1730-1803)

Frederick Hervey was the forty-eighth Bishop of Derry and was, without doubt, totally ill-suited for a life as 'a man of the cloth'.

For one thing, he had been accused of being an atheist. For another, he was frequently bored, so when he was compelled to perform his duties as bishop he would find new ways of entertaining himself. A memorable example occurred in 1758, when he summoned all of his clergymen to participate in a jumping contest to see which of his clergy could jump the highest. For this he designed a race that involved jumping over all the hedgerows and gates between one church and another, about 2 miles away.

A few years later he thought of another 'jolly jape' to amuse himself. This came about when a much sought-after clerical post became vacant in his diocese. He then wrote to all of the fattest clergymen he could find and invited them over for an extremely sumptuous dinner. Once they had all eaten and arose with full bellies from the table, the bishop, keeping a very straight face, announced that the post would be awarded to the winner of a cross-country race that would be held immediately. Sitting on a horse, Hervey waved a flag to signify the race had started and the vicars slowly waddled off. But Hervey had signposted the race through a nearby bog. One by one they fell flat on their faces and wallowed helplessly in the mud, much to the bishop's delight.

Another story tells how he once scattered flour outside a female guests room in order to enjoy her embarrassment at seeing her nocturnal vistor's footprints.

During his European travels, and especially during his frequent visits to Rome, the bishop was known to walk around wearing a broad-brimmed white hat, many gold chains and red breeches, in deliberate contrast to what a Church of Ireland bishop was expected to wear. He was fond of riding in red velvet breeches and a white sombrero trimmed with purple to match the colour of his stockings.

The bishop also hated the sound of church bells. One day, in Siena, a religious procession passed beneath his hotel window with bells tinkling away. Hervey took exception to this and poured a large pot of pasta over them.

He was in his beloved Italy when he died in July 1893. He had collapsed outside a small cottage but the Catholic occupant refused to let the flamboyantly dressed Hervey inside, insisting that he was a heretic. So poor Hervey drew his last breath in a stable nearby. This was not the end of this saga though, as superstitious Italian sailors refused to allow his coffin upon their boats and it was up to the British Minister in Naples to come up with the idea of placing the coffin in a packing case with 'Antique Statue' stamped on it, so that his body could be transported back to Ireland.

THOMAS GISBORNE GORDON (1851-1935)

A more than capable second-row forward who played against England in 1877 and gained a further two caps the following season, he is almost certainly the only player to have played international rugby with only one hand. He lost his right hand in a shooting accident as a youngster.

He made his debut in the first rugby international played between 15-a-side teams: England v. Ireland at The Oval on 5 February 1877, a game which England won by two goals to nil. Prior to this, rugby had been played with 20-a-side teams.

He won his second cap against Scotland before completing his international career against the English in 1878 at Lansdowne Road in the first rugby test played at the venue. Interestingly, all previous matches had been held at the Leinster Cricket Club in Rathmines.

HENRY BERESFORD, 3RD MARQUIS OF WATERFORD (1811-59)

Known as 'The Mad Marquis', Henry Beresford had the distinction of finishing a distant last as a jockey in the 1840 Grand National. He was apparently so hung-over on the morning of the race that he needed a couple of bottles of brandy 'to restore the equilibrium'. Sadly it did not have the required effect as he trailed in last of the runners to complete the course.

Waterford spent a small fortune on various stunts. When life became dull (it appears that happened on a regular basis) he would try out a new prank. He once bought a large quantity of gin and stood in the street, handing out free drinks to anyone who looked to be unhappy. Needless to say, it did not take long before a drunken riot broke out and the still-giggling Waterford was arrested.

He is also responsible for the phrase 'painting the town red' entering the English language. This occurred when, while riding back drunk from a race meeting with his friends, he decided not to pay the toll-keeper to open the gate. Whilst arguing with him, Waterford noticed some pots of red paint and with the help of his equally drunk friends then proceeded to run riot and paint the toll bar, several adjoining buildings and the poor toll-keeper red. Hardly surprisingly, the following day there was uproar, and despite the now sobered up Waterford offering to pay for all the damage, the group were still brought to trial before the Derby Assize Court. They were found not guilty of riot, but were each fined £100 (the equivalent of nearly £11,000 at todays rates).

He once filled the first-class carriage of a train bound for a race meeting with chimney sweeps, simply to see the looks on the faces of the other first-class passengers.

On another occasion he was summoned to appear at court on a charge of driving his horse and carriage through a crowded thoroughfare at a reckless and dangerous speed. He arrived for the hearing on horseback, rode up to the court house steps and demanded to be let in. The horse, he said, was a witness for the defence. He insisted that the horse was to be cross-examined 'because only he knows how fast he was going'. The Judge, knowing Waterford's reputation for lunacy, decided that in the best of interests of everyone he should acquit Waterford in order not to create yet another potential riot.

Waterford was very fond of showing off on his horse. On several occasions he charged up the steps of the Kilkenny Hunt Clubhouse in an attempt to be allowed into the bar. He also had an aversion to the fashionable dandies of the day, who would promenade up and down the smarter streets of Dublin in their fine clothes. So Waterford dressed up as a coalman and drove a coal cart up and down the streets, making sure that he stirred as much coal dust as possible.

Even his friends were not safe from his japes, as a house guest once found out when he found himself in bed with a donkey. He once did some house-sitting for some friends who were going on holiday. Upon their return they discovered that he had shot out all the eyes of all of the family portraits and that there were bullet holes in all the ceilings. He was just as bad at his home in Curraghmore, County Waterford, where he shot holes in the mouths of various family ancestors portraits and then stuck cigars in them.

Despite that some of his jokes inevitably ended up with some form of destruction, he always made good the damage. There was the time when he decided to sit on all the hats in a milliner's shop. The milliner burst into tears and declared that she was a ruined woman. The Marquis told her that he just couldn't resist the temptation and handed her a handsome cheque.

One evening, he hired eight cabs and a group of musicians to sit on the roofs and play while they were driven in procession around the streets. Waterford took the reins of the leading cab, inviting anyone and everyone to climb in and have a ride. The evening came to a swifter end than he intended, however, when three of the musicians fell off the roof and had to be taken to hospital.

Despite everything, he himself managed to survive all his wild pranks, only to break his neck in a mundane riding accident in 1859.

LADY ELEANOR BUTLER (1739-1829) AND SARAH PONSONBY (1755-1831)

In 1774, Lady Eleanor, the daughter of an Irish peer, and Sarah Ponsonby, her kinswoman, met at a Kilkenny dinner party and were instantly attracted to each other. Lady Eleanor was 39, Miss Ponsonby ten years younger. They then formulated a plan for a private rural retreat, rather than face the possibility of being forced into marriages. They eloped together in April 1778. Their families hunted them down and tried to make them change their minds, but they refused. Their decision to withdraw from the world and set up home together in a little Welsh village led to them becoming known as the 'Ladies of Llangollen'.

They living in complete seclusion apart from Flirt the dog and Mrs Tatters, the cat. They did not spend a single day away from their little farmhouse until their deaths fifty years later. Always dressed in men's clothes, Lady Eleanor and Sarah Ponsonby occupied themselves by tending their lovingly planted garden and taking long, brisk walks.

Sarah Ponsonby herself described their idyllic existence in a letter to a friend:

In the mornings after breakfast I try to improve myself in drawing. My beloved is also improving herself, though this is scarce possible, in Italian. After dinner she reads aloud to me till nine o'clock when we generally retire to our dressing rooms where we generally employ ourselves until twelve.

Rather surprisingly, during this particular period of history romantic friendships between women were actually approved of. Although of course, there was to be never any mention of any 'tipping the velvet' behaviour.

They both lived happily together for the rest of their lives; their books and glassware carried both sets of initials and their letters were jointly signed.

Eleanor Butler died in 1829 and Sarah Ponsonby died two years later.

ANASTACIA ARCHDEACON

Monkstown Castle in County Cork was finally finished in 1636 by an Anastacia Archdeacon as a surprise for her husband, who was off fighting in the Spanish Wars. On the day he returned he thought his lands had been invaded and immediately started firing on it before his wife came out and explained what had actually happened.

She was obviously a very astute woman, as the whole castle was built for the cost of just fourpence. Apparently she not only insisted that her workmen buy all their food and clothing from her stores, but she also charged them for the use of water and the latrines. In this way she ended up recovering all but fourpence on her outlay.

THOMAS LEGGE (?-1808)

Born in Donaghdee in Ulster, the son of a wealthy shipowner, Thomas Legge looked set for a comfortable and prosperous life. But it appeared that young Legge had neither the interest nor temperament for a life in commerce, he craved excitement and adventure. So one day he just left without a word and made his way to Liverpool, where he joined a Royal Navy ship bound for India.

He quickly realised that the disciplined life as a member of His Majesty's Navy was not for him and he jumped ship as soon as they disembarked in Madras. Uncertain of what to do and rapidly running out of money, he supported himself by begging and singing Irish folk songs. Salvation came in the name of a Major Sangster, who suggested that Legge should join him as a mercenary in the service of the Jat Rana of Gohad. He quickly rose through the ranks to become a cavalry officer and was highly regarded by his employer. But after a couple of years, Legge's restless spirit took over and he decided to leave for a new adventure, this time ,Kabul in Afghanastan. Using his new-found expertise he trained his new host's army in Europen military tactics and it was here that he first got interested in Indian alchemy and divination. Over the next twelve years he criss-crossed India offering his services as a mercenary. He very nearly settled down after marrying a local woman in Badakshan but his nomadic spirit moved him on.

One day, after shooting himself in the foot after cleaning his rifle, he hobbled over to a nearby British camp for his wound to be treated. The doctor who treated him was a Captain Todd, who was fascinated by this strange Irishman with his endless supply of stories about his travels. As Captain Todd quickly came to realise, Legge was also quite mad. He believed that he had discovered the Garden of Eden deep in the Hindu Kush: 'a beautiful garden filled with delicious fruit with piles of gold bricks at one end and silver at the other'. He also claimed that he had taken tea with John the Baptist.

A few days after leaving the camp, Legge, now fully recovered (physically), must have had some sort of episode. He threw away all of his clothes and belongings and took up residence in a deserted tomb, proclaiming himself a fakir. Sitting outside cross-legged in his loincloth, he survived on the good will of passers-by, but after an ill judged fast in early 1808 he caught a fever and died a few days later.

JOSHUA JACOB (1805-77)

Now remembered as the leader of a rather bonkers and somewhat eccentric sect that came to be known as 'the White Quakers', Jacob was born in Clonmel in about 1805.

After a very successful business career as a grocer in Dublin, he was 'disowned' by the Society of Friends, of which he was a member, due to his increasingly bizarre preaching and odd behaviour. Undeterred, in 1838, he quickly gathered a few disciples and started his own eccentric sect.

The sect members dressed only in white, destroyed everything ornamental in their houses, and had compulsory prayer meetings three times a day. Astonishingly, the sect quickly grew and in a very short time had spread to Mountmellick, Clonmel and Waterford. They also issued a series of rather confusing tracts entitled *The Progress of Truth*.

In 1849 he gathered his followers into probably the first commune in Ireland at Newlands, near Dublin. They only ate bruised corn and by all accounts seemed very content. However, there is a newspaper report that in 1856 six members of the group, 'both men and women, attempted to parade around Newlands in a condition of entire nudity.'

Joshua appeared to start suffering from delusions shortly after and the community at Newlands slowly disbanded and drifted away.

He died on 15 February 1877, aged about 72, and was buried in Glasnevin Cemetery.

GEORGE THOMAS (1756-1802)

Born in Roscrea, County Tipperary, this most unlikely individual became a ruler of his own kingdom in India.

Working on the docks at Youghal, he was press-ganged into the British Navy, spending three years at sea before he managed to desert in 1781 when the ship was docked in Bombay. He made off with some provisions and the Captain's horse, and made his way to Madras.

Following a fight during his first night in Madras, he was offered a job as a 'bouncer' for one of the city's many brothels. With his red hair and pale skin he quickly became well-known in the area. He then met and fell in love with an Indian Princess, the Begum Samru of Sardhana. At her request he moved to Sardhana, where he then trained and put together a group of soldiers to serve under her. All was going well for Thomas until he was caught in flagrante delicto with one of the princess's many maids, Faced with public castration or exile, he wisely chose the latter and fled.

He then transferred his allegiance to a sworn enemy of the princess, a fellow called Appo Rao, who was a Mahrattan chieftain. Appo Rao took a shine to the Irishman, and after a couple of years he rewarded his loyalty by gifting him a swathe of land in Rohtak, where with Appo Rao's blessing, Thomas decided to create his own independent kingdom. Thomas established a mint and released his own rupees of his new kingdom; the rupees even had a likeness of himself stamped on one side. By all accounts he was a good ruler and successfully put an end to most of the corruption that was rife in the area.

Nonetheless, it appeared that he still could not keep it in his trousers. In early 1800 he reneged on a marriage promise to a young French woman – unbeknownst to him, she was the young cousin of General Pierre Cullier-Perron, who promptly captured and imprisoned him.

He was eventually released and, still a wealthy man, he intended to move back to Ireland and enjoy his fortune. But he caught a fever after bedding a French officer's wife and died whilst making his way down the Ganges River in 1802.

His story became the basis of Rudyard Kipling's excellent novel *The Man Who Would Be King*, which later became a halfway decent film with Sean Connery and Michael Caine.

GEORGE HANGER, BARON COLERAINE (1751-1824)

By the time Hanger was just 22, he had fought with three regiments, been wounded in the American War of

Independence, reached the rank of Colonel, fought three duels and married a gypsy girl – who then ran off with a tinker. It is hardly surprisingly that, after all of this, Hanger decided to settle down and start to enjoy life. And enjoy life he did!

Due to his exploits on the battlefields he was summoned to court and quickly became firm friends with the Prince Regent. Hanger then became known as somewhat of a dandy, and is said to have been the first man in England to wear a silk coat. But the ever-restless Hanger, perhaps missing the adrenaline of fighting in the army, became known for indulging in increasingly daft wagers, which in turn meant he ended up broke.

One particular bet was on a 10-mile race between a gaggle of geese and a flock of turkeys, a wager he eventually lost when his turkeys lost interest and ran away in the first mile of the race. This experience cost Hanger £500 and, coupled with other ridiculous bets, he found himself in King's Bench Gaol after living way beyond his means for more than a decade. Poor Hanger languished there in considerable squalor for nearly a year and a half before his debts were paid off and he was allowed to leave.

He must have had a 'Road to Damascus' moment, as he appeared to be a totally different man upon his release. He then surprised everybody by deciding to become a coal merchant – he became rather good at it, too – and was quickly solvent again. With the successive deaths of his two older brothers, he was suddenly left with a title, Baron Coleraine. He refused to use it and insisted on being addressed as 'just plain old George Hanger, if you please.'

Revelling in his new life as a fully-fledged man of the people, the fourth and last Lord Coleraine decided to share his wisdom with the public by writing a book, which he called *The Life, Adventures, and Opinions of Col. George Hanger.* With the emphasis firmly placed on the third of these, most of his advice was directed at the ladies. For example, the then current fashion for large, loose gowns was applauded by Hanger as being perfect to conceal both the bulk of a Mary Harney and the swag of anyone wishing to indulge in a little shoplifting.

Girls considering elopement were similarly advised to leave by a window not the door, thereby establishing themselves in a heroic role and showing their men they were full of 'spirit, courage and spunk'. Beggar-women were also encouraged to find themselves blind men as companions, and Hanger frequently made trips into the countryside to persuade village priests to effect the necessary introductions.

Finally, said Hanger, the government should bring in a new tax payable by any Scotsman who strayed over the border for more than six months at a time, although just where the inspiration came for that one is rather hard to say.

George Hanger died of a 'convulsive fit' on March 31 1824. His gravestone describes him as: 'a practical Christian, as far as his frail nature did allow him so to be.'

COLONEL JOHN OGLE

During the summer of 1797, a Colonel John Ogle walked 53 miles from Dublin to Dundalk to win a wager. The sum in question? One penny!

ALEXANDER MILLAR (1795-?)

In 1823, this 28-year-old County Down convict escaped the penal colony of Van Diemens Land (Tasmania) by stowing aboard the sealing ship *The Caroline*. After the ship had reached its port of call, Millar then took his chance and fled. What he did not realise, however, was that the ship had docked at Maquarie Island – a bleak, inhospitable place with no other inhabitants to speak of, apart from seals. Lots of seals. Millar then spent the next two years permanently cold and hungry before deciding that this was a dreadful price to pay for freedom.

When another sealing ship arrived, he asked them to take him back to Hobart with them. On his return to Tasmania, the now grateful Millar received fifty lashes and was then sent to a nearby island penal settlement. You would have thought that Millar would have now learnt his lesson, settled down and served out the remainder of his sentence. Apparently not.

The doughty Millar next tried to stowaway on a ship that was heading back to mainland Europe, but he got on the wrong ship and was arrested once again. He was then sentenced to six months in a chain gang and a month on the treadmill.

He did eventually escape, however, in 1845, over twenty years after his first attempt. He appears to have run off with a Baptist missionary called Brian, and was never seen again.

GEORGE FITZGERALD (1746-86)

George Robert Fitzgerald, a descendant of the great Irish Desmond family, was a walking volcano. Incredibly short-tempered, he lived to fight.

He first drew blood at the age of just 15, when a man dared to insult the young Fitzgerald to win a bet and approached him in a coffee house shouting, 'I smell an Irishman.' Fitzgerald promptly drew a knife and cut off his antagonist's nose, saying, 'Then you shall never smell another.'

After building up a reputation as a fearless duellist, he met his match in a duel with an army officer. Fitzgerald was shot in the head and, as the surgeon was trying his best to remove the bullet lodged in his skull, Fitzgerald, in agony and streaming with blood, was shouting and cursing at him not to damage his wig.

Bad tempers seemed to be compulsory in the Fitzgerald family. When George's father heard that his son had been shot, he was so upset that he ran his sword through the first man who offered him his condolences.

Although badly scarred for life, the young Fitzgerald survived, but became more unpredictable than ever, probably a legacy of his head injury. He grew adept at picking quarrels and provoking duels on the flimsiest of pretexts. When he fancied an argument he would lash out at complete strangers on the street or snatch their rings or watches; once he shot off a man's wig. If he failed to pick a fight in a bar or theatre he would stand in the middle of a narrow street waiting for someone to jostle him.

Whilst in Paris he skewered with his rapier a man who had accidentally stepped on his dog. On this occasion, however, an enraged mob of Frenchmen followed him back to his lodgings, trashed his carriage and killed his valet.

By the age of 27, Fitzgerald had fought in nearly forty duels. He was now an expert marksman and he was proud to boast that he could hit a target on any part of the human body to within a fly's wingspan.

In 1786 Fitzgerald had his final duel, in which he shot and killed a neighbour of his, a Colonel McDonnell. The authorities in County Mayo finally acted, having become weary of the 38 year old psychopath continually using his family name and connections to flout the law. He was tried and sentenced to hang for murder.

On the day of his execution Fitzgerald drank a whole bottle of port and was surprisingly chatty on the scaffold. However, the rope broke and he fell to the ground. He got up, gave a bow to the crowd and said 'You see that I am once more among you.' The second attempt proved to be more successful.

Fitzgerald left a young daughter, who survived her father by eight years before dying suddenly and unexpectedly. It was said that she keeled over and died of shock after reading a particularly gruesome report on her father's execution in the *Gentleman's Magazine*.

THE INDEPENDENT SOVIET REPUBLIC OF LIMERICK (1919)

Did you know that, for twelve heady days, the city of Limerick and its surrounding area was a self-declared soviet republic?

At the start of the Irish War of Independence, as a protest against the British Army having declared the city a

'Special Military Area', Limerick called a general strike and declared itself a soviet state. During the twelve days (15–27 April 1919) the short-lived soviet printed its own money and newspapers, and organised a co-operative for the distribution of food.

This prompted a media frenzy as dozens of reporters descended on Limerick to write about what was going on. *The Chicago Tribune* reported with a straight face that 'when the bells of the nearby St Munchin's Church tolled the Angelus, all the red-badged Soviet soldiers stood and blessed themselves.'

The whole thing was not as crazy as it initially sounds, as there was a soviet republic in Hungary and several German towns, as well as mass factory occupations in Italy. And a few years later, in 1921, the Arigna mines in Leitrim were taken over and run as a soviet for two months before the workers got a pay rise and handed back the mine to its owners.

Anyway back to the Limerick Soviet, which was always going to end in tears. As it appears that they even went as far as applying to join the Soviet Union itself, but someone lost the paperwork.

SUPPLE JACK

Some time towards the end of the fifteenth century in Castlegregory, County Kerry, there lived a man known as 'Supple Jack'. A small, lithe fellow he would suddenly turn up in villages barefoot wearing an old, red soldier's tunic and a pair of raggedy old trousers that he had cut down to make a pair of shorts.

He was possibly the most famous fox trapper in the county. He also had a most novel way of catching them. Using a bunch of blackthorn switches, he would weave them with sharp thorns to create a long stick. He would then crawl down into the fox's den and draw out the young cubs by entangling the rods in their fur and pulling them, in the manner of a fisherman.

He was thought to be dead after a tunnel collapsed behind him on a particularly wet night, but somehow managed to survive entombed for three days before being rescued.

His demise came about, somewhat ironically, when a shelf displaying a number of fox skulls unexpectedly collapsed and one of the skulls grazed poor Jack's head. The wound became infected, which led to a fever and then to his death.

DAN DONNELLY (1788-1820)

The larger than life Dan Donnelly was perhaps the most famous sportsman of his time. Originally working as a carpenter, he quickly gained a reputation as a 'fair man' but 'handy with his fists'. There are a number of apocryphal tales about his early life in Dublin, one of which involved him coming to the aid of a young girl who was being attacked by a couple of sailors. Another has him carrying the body of an old lady who had died of typhoid to the local cemetary after the undertaker had refused to assist in the burial.

Compared to most modern-day boxers he was not particularly big, standing just under 6ft and weighing about 15 stone. But what was extraordinary about him is that he only ever had three bouts but was victorious in all of them. The fight that cemented his fame was against the leading prizefighter of the day, an Englishman called George Cooper. The fight, which took place in Donnelly's Hollow in the Curragh on the afternoon of 13 November 1815, began shortly after 10 a.m. in front of over 20,000 spectators. After eleven rounds of an extremely bruising and bloody fight, he won with a final punch that broke his opponent's jaw

On retiring from boxing, he bought and ran a number of pubs, the only one surviving today being Fallons Capstan Bar in Merchants Quay, Dublin. Sadly he drifted into a life of alcoholism. According to Donnelly's biographer, Patrick Myler, his eventual demise came about when he drank

> an almost incredible number of tumblers of whiskey punch at one sitting. He then swallowed half a bucket of cold water, while in a state of profuse perspiration, after the aforesaid tumblers, he burst a blood vessel and departed this life.

Upon his death, thousands of mourners followed the funeral cortege to the cemetary at Bully's Acre in Kilmainham. His boxing gloves were carried on a silk cushion at the head of the procession, and some of the mourners unhitched the horses from the hearse and pulled it themselves out to Kilmainham.

There you would think that the story would end. But following Donnelly's death a series of unfortunate events took place. Iin the early nineteenth century the medical profession was making great strides in understanding the workings of the human body, and as a result needed fresh human cadavers. This inadvertently led to a rise in grave-robbing. Donnelly's well meaning friends stood vigil by the graveside in order to prevent this from happening. But, as *Carrick's*

Morning Post described, they got drunk: 'The severity of the weather prompted them to make too frequent libations on the tomb of the departed champion and disabled them from perceiving or opposing those riflers of the House of Death.'

Donnelly's corpse was taken to a local surgeon a Dr Hall. He was appalled that they could have done such a thing to a great champion. The doctor then insisted Donnelly should be returned to the graveyard immediately, but just before the body could be removed Dr Hall cut off the champion's right arm, claiming that he needed to study it later.

Donnelly's arm then spent the next century on the move. First it was as an exhibit at a medical school in Edinburgh, where it was lacquered and used in anatomy lectures. Then it was in a travelling circus and journeyed all across Europe. When the circus closed and started selling off its assets, the eagle-eyed Belfast bookmaker, Hugh 'Texas' McAlevey, bought in and then sold it on to a Tom Donnelly (no relation), who completed the circle by giving it to 'The Hide-Out pub in Kilcullen, near the site of Donnelly's greatest triumph.

BUTTY SUGRUE (1924-77)

Probably best remembered as the promoter behind the 1972 fight between Muhammad Ali and Al Lewis in Dublin, but before that he laid claim to being the 'Strongest Man in Ireland'.

Born in Killorglin, near Gortnascarry, in 1924, he was one of six children. Even as a child he was exceptionally strong for his age: he got the name 'Butty' whilst working as a turf cutter where he would entertain his fellow workers with impromptu strongman shows.

He then joined up with Duffy's Circus where he proved to be a natural showman, and it was there that he was first billed as 'Ireland's Strongest Man'

As part of his act he would lift four 56lb weights attached to a cart axel, much like a weightlifter would. But he always finished his act by dragging a cart filled with ten men around the big top with his teeth.

Leaving the circus in the early 1950s, he reinvented himself as a wrestler and began to promote tours around the country. Heand brought well-known boxers such as Joe Louis and Henry Cooper to Ireland.

They did not appear to have been particularly profitable, so in 1962 he decided to move to London, where he took over a couple of pubs, the Wellington in Shepherd Bush and the Admiral Nelson in Kilburn. His natural exuberance and his love of being in the public eye quickly made him a local celebrity. He reinforced this by a number of appearances on television, where he attracted even more publicity with his feats of strength.

The eccentric Sugrue seemed to be permanently in the news, one occasion being when he somehow convinced one of his barmen to try and break the record for the most days buried alive. The barman in question, a Mike Meaney from Ballyporeen, did indeed break the record by being under-ground for 61 days. There was also the famous incident when he pulled a London bus up Kilburn High Road with one hand whilst pushing a baby in a pram with the other.

Flush with success, he decided to bring Muhammed Ali – perhaps then the most famous man in the world – to Ireland for a 'super fight'. The bout was held at Croke Park on 19 July 1971. Ali won the fight easily against the Irish challenger Al 'Blue' Lewis. Sadly the event turned out to be a disaster, everything that could go wrong seemingly did.

The first thing that occurred was that no one had thought to supply boxing gloves, so somebody was despatched on the day of the fight to scour sport shops all over Dublin to buy some professional standard boxing gloves. Secondly, due to the lax security on the day of the fight it was estimated that half of the 18,000 spectators got in free. Poor old Butty was said to have lost nearly £30,000.

He seemed to fade out of the news after that, but appeared again for all the wrong reasons in 1977. After ordering a new fridge, he refused help from the delivery men and then had a heart attack trying to carry it upstairs.

CLOTWORTHY SKEFFINGTON, THE EARL OF MASSERENE (1743-1805)

For the first twenty-five years of his life, until he inherited his father's title and became the 2nd Earl of Masserene, the splendidly named Clotworthy Skeffington led a quiet and mostly blameless life

But on a visit to Paris in 1741, he managed to get involved in a disasterous business venture that spectacularly failed when his business partners ran off, leaving poor Clotworthy imprisoned for debt. Faced with the choice of admitting his guilt and paying up or going to prison, he stubbornly refused to pay and and chose to be incarcerated in La Force prison for twenty-five years, after which time, according to French law, his debts would be cancelled. It seemed that he did not have suffer much, as due to a £4,000 a year bribe he was given an extremely comfortable suite of rooms where his friends and mistresses were only too pleased to visit and dine with him on wonderful dinners served by his private chef.

Romance blossomed, as he fell in love with and married Marie-Anne Barcier, the beautiful daughter of the prison governor. Determined to help him escape she put her liberty at risk on two occasions until finally in 1789, after nearly twenty years in prison he was eventually released.

He returned to Antrim Castle, his seat in Ireland, but his experiences in France had left him convinced that a revolutionary war was coming, and thus he created his own private army to defend himself.There was one glaring flaw to his plan, however, as he did not have any guns or ammunition. This did not seem to bother him at all; he trained his soldiers to mimic the sound of musket shots by clapping their hands . He also invented new drills with names such as Serpentine and Eel-in-the-Mud, which involved sequences of bizarre hand signals. Sadly for our friend, the official call to incorporate his crack unit into the militia never came.

He was very self conscious about his size, being rather small and thin. He had a solution to this; every morning he would walk up and down his courtyard with his arms crossed tightly in front of him, hugging his shoulders. He took the view that if he suppressed the growth of one part of the body it would bulge out elsewhere and he would grow broad and tall

Another of his eccentricities was to dine outside –not in the garden, but on the roof. It was better for the digestion so he thought. He would request that the dining table, complete with all the china and cutlery, the requisite number of dining chairs and of course the food for the dinner, were rbought up, by means of a complicated winch and pulley system. Once the party was seated at the relocated table and about to start their alfresco meal, Clotworthy more often than not declared himself unsatisfied and ordered everything back inside. One neighbour after being invited to one of his dinners was reported to have said, 'I had previously heard a report that he was a lunatic, but I then thought that if he was a lunatic, he was the pleasantest one I had ever met.'

Later, when one of his wife's pet dogs fell ill, she was distraught with grief, convinced that it was dying. Clotworthy disagreed, saying that he had seen many dog deaths. When his wife would not believe him, he lay on his back on the carpet and gave a lengthy impression of a dying dog to prove her wrong. When his wife's favourite dog did eventually die, he decreed thatall the local dogs were invited to its funeral at Antrim Castle. Fifty of them were provided with white scarves and acted as a guard of honour.

When his wife died in 1800, he married one of his servants, who with the help of her family managed to relieve poor Clotworthy of much of his wealth before his own death in 1805.

WILLIAM FRANCIS BRINSLEY LE POER TRENCH, EARL OF CLANCARTY (1911-95)

Prior to inheriting his earldom in 1976 as the 8th Earl of Clancarty, Le Poer Trench worked as an advertising salesman for a gardening magazine, and edited a magazine called *Flying Saucer Review*.

He immediately took advantage of his new position in the House of Lords to form the first official Parliamentary

All-Party UFO Study Group. He did this in order to assist himself in his lifelong bid to prove his theory: that the majority of unidentified flying objects arrive here not from outer space, but from secret bases located deep inside the Earth, which is actually hollow. He was convinced that aliens were living amongst us and would frequently kidnap human beings in order to brainwash them. Following this procedure, the aliens would be returned to the 'Upper Earth' through a series of seven or eight tunnels, where they would assimilate back into society as programmed agents (though he did have the good grace to admit that he had not been down there himself). Trench also believed that the lost continent of Atlantis actually once existed and that these tunnels were probably constructed all over the world by the Atlanteans before the aliens took them over.

He also wrote a number of books on the subject with titles such as *The Sky People*. All of these are long out of print.

In 1964 he helped set up Contact International, which was intended to allow fellow UFOlogists from around the world to share extraterrestrial sightings. He had originally wanted to call the organisation the International Sky Scouts, but the real Boy Scouts were somewhat unimpressed and threatened legal action. For some reason he was particularly popular in Japan and was invited there in 1966 by the Cosmic Brotherhood – a cult that worshipped flying saucers, to participate in a ceremony on top of a 'sun pyramid'. The Cosmic Brotherhood wanted to celebrate the fact that an alien in a flying saucer had visited Earth thousands of years ago to show early humans how to grow certain vegetables. He also claimed that he could trace his descent from 63,000bc, when beings from other planets had first landed on Earth.

He was also obsessed with UFO propulsion systems and claimed that he had a number of top secret meetings with a high ranking Honda executive to discuss the technical specifications of a crashed UFO's propulsion mechanism. So, if we ever see a flying Honda Civic in a car showroom, we will know who to thank.

A. ATKINSON

Living in Moate, County Westmeath, Atkinson had a Martin Luther King moment when he was given details of a world-changing of philosophy during a dream. He felt compelled to write down and tell the world and, in 1812, he published the mysteriously titled *The Roll of a Tennis-Ball through a Moral World* to a less than enthusiastic public.

Not at all put off with the deafening silence that surrounded his book, he then left his wife and six children in order to travel around Ireland, seeking would-be patrons to bear the cost of a new book. He would put any new subscribers into one of four columns, ranging from 'generous' to 'mean'. Daniel O'Connor and Lord Meath were added to the 'generous' column whilst the 'mean column' seemed to be made up entirely of the priesthood.

When the new book, *The Irish Tourist*, was finally published, people appeared to be more interested in the introduction than the contents of the book. For the introduction was where Atkinson had listed, with various waspish comments, all of his subscribers in the various columns.

WILLIAM THOMPSON (1775-1833)

A few years after the French Revolution, the young William Thompson decided to visit Paris. He was so taken with all of the new concepts that republican France offered that upon his return to Ireland, he was a changed man.

Walking around the local villages, he would stop and harangue anyone who cared to listen with his manifesto of free schooling for all, equal rights for Catholics and (most damningly of all) votes for women. He quickly became known as the 'Red Republican'.

William inherited a 1,700-acre estate in Carhoogariff, West Cork, after his father's death in 1814. Refusing to become an absentee landlord, he decided to live on the estate and one of the first things he did was to reduce his tenants rent, stating that it was fundamentally wrong for a landowner to profit from the toil of his tenants. Sadly this laudable act backfired on him a couple of years later, as due to an accumulation of debts, he was forced to sell some of his land.

In the meantime, he had been corresponding with the London-based philosopher Jeremy Bentham. He quickly became a devotee of Bentham's belief in ultilitarianism and was determined that 'happiness' ought to be distributed more evenly.

Back in Ireland, in 1825 he co-published the highly controversial *An Appeal of One Half of the Human Race* with the Germaine Greer of the time, Anna Doyle Wheeler. It was the first to champion the need for an increased role for women in society.

Thompson was both a teetotaller and vegetarian; he ate only turnips and potatoes. Following this strict diet and way of life, he explained, helped him to concentrate more on his reading and writing. He did, however, have one guilty pleasure: honey. On his estate in Carhoogariff he had a number of beehives, of which he was very proud. He would only eat the honey sparingly, but once he found a small field mouse stuck in one of the hives and licked the animal clean before releasing it.

Always prone to bad health, he died aged 57 in 1833, and leaving no immediate heirs, as he was unmarried. Despite being well-known as an atheist and very critical of priests (he was fond of calling them 'ghost dealers in creed and spiritual brimstone'), his family went against his wishes by giving him a Church burial. He did have the last laugh, however, as his will contained a number of eccentric requests, one of which was that his body had to be dug back up because his ribs were to be 'tipped with silver' to present a 'fashionable look', and his skull was to be cleaned and polished and then gifted to a well-known phrenologist. Wrangling over the rest of the will meant the case dragged on for 25 years – possibly the longest such case in Irish history. By the time judgement was given, legal costs had virtually wiped out its value.

MATHEW ROBINSON, LORD ROKEBY (1712-1800)

When Matthew Robinson inherited the title of Lord Rokeby from his uncle, the Archbishop of Armagh, he was already 81 years of age.

As an ex-Member of Parliament he had strong views on just about everything. He was a fervent believer in the health-giving properties of fresh air and exercise. He walked everywhere, and rather considerately took along a carriage for the servants who did not share his stamina. At home he never lit a fire and the windows were always left open.

Rokeby's appearance was equally odd. He had a beard that reached his knees and his moustache was long enough for him to be able to tuck the ends under his arms.

His diet consisted of 'beef, over which boiled water had been poured'. He would also refuse to drink tea or coffee and believed that the eating of 'exotics' such as wheat was wicked. He experimented with burnt peas and beans instead of coffee, and always ate standing up at a tiny table designed just to take one plate.

The other obsession he had was the use of water, and he recommended that everyone should drink at least a gallon a day. He built drinking fountains across his estate and would reward his tenants with a sixpence if he saw them drinking from them.

Every morning he would bathe his eyes in salt water, and then spend the rest of the day immersed in the stuff. Before he built himself a bath house, he would be frequently found in the many ponds around the estate. On more than a few occasions he had to be dragged out to dry land, unconscious due to the cold. When it was built, the bath house was fitted with a glass front which allowed 'the water to be rendered tepid by the rays of the sun'. The neighbours and servants got used to seeing him dart from his house down the garden towards the bath. The sight was something to behold. He was always naked, his beard tucked under his arm, and he was followed by his barking dogs. In the bath house he would sit up to his neck in his favourite liquid whilst eating his meals, entertaining visitors and writing wonderfully odd political pamphlets.

A difficult man, he had no time for doctors; indeed, when he was dying he told his nephew that if he called a doctor he would disinherit him. It seems that his cure for just about everything was to never light a fire and open all the windows.

He was also convinced that the Bank of England would collapse at any moment. He was so convinced that it would occur that he wagered £10 on this happening. Part of his will stated that the bet would continue on through his heirs. So, after over 200 years, this is perhaps the oldest continuously running bet ever.

DR AHMED BORONBAD/ PADDY JOYCE

Suddenly appearing sometime in the late 1880s, a Turkish man resplendent in traditional dress and a long black beard immediately caused a stir on the streets of Dublin. Who was this mysterious man and what on earth was he doing here?

He claimed to be a Turkish refugee by the name of Dr Ahmed Boronbad, and he was looking to open the first Turkish Baths in Ireland. He was, by all accounts, a natural salesman and very quickly convinced local businessmen, lawyers and doctors of the very real benefits that a Turkish Baths would bring Dublin. With his new-found friends' blessing, he was then introduced to a number of Irish members of Parliament who helped him receive the initial funding for the new and very exclusive Turkish Bath House, which was to be built at Bachelor's Walk.

The premise for the Bath House was quite simple. Boronbad would build a number of hot and cold seawater baths, with a large underground boiler supplying the necessary heat for the hot ones. Work began and the best marble was brought in and pipes were laid. The problem was that Boronbad kept running out of money due to his habit of constantly changing his mind about where things should go during the construction. Undeterred he would return to Parliament and petition for more funding. Due to his influential friends, the funding was never refused. Until one fateful day ...

On the evening before he would visit Parliament for yet more money, he decided, as was his habit, to throw a splendid party at the (still partially built) baths for all his important friends. This particular evening proved to be the last. Hosting a group of thirty dignitaries, Boronbad had surpassed himself as a host: there was a small orchestra playing, a bevy of beautiful women and a seemingly never-ending supply of the very best of wines. The evening took a turn for the worse when the elderly Sir John Hamilton decided to take his leave and go home. For some reason, he opened the wrong door and fell into the now bitterly cold seawater bath. In a scene worthy of a *Carry On* film, another dozen of Dublin's finest also fell in trying to rescue him. If that wasn't bad enough, worse was to follow. After they had been dragged out of the pool, they stood around in sodden clothing only to discover that the only dry clothing to be found was the traditional Turkish clothing worn by the attendants. Dublin was then treated to the spectacle of a swarm of damp MPs dressed in ill-fitting but colourful Turkish clothing making their way back to their respective homes.

This particular story now takes another bizarre turn. Boronbad had met and fallen in love with a Miss Hartigan, the sister of a respectable Dublin surgeon. It appears that the no doubt sensible Miss Hartigan rebuffed his approaches and refused to speak to him unless he shaved off his beard and wore 'Christian clothing'. By now things were not looking too good for our Turkish friend, as funds had dried up and he was living on what was left of his credit. The mysterious Turk was finally unmasked when, in order to win Miss Hartigan's hand, he shaved off his beard, got rid of the Turkish costume and announced to her that he was in fact Paddy Joyce from Kilkenny.

Unfortunately, there is no record of her response – or indeed what eventually happened to them.

JAMES JOYCE (1882-1942)

The acclaimed author of *Ulysses* was an unashamed underwear fetishist. He was aroused by just looking at his wife Norah's knickers, and insisted she left them around the house.

Not content with keeping his peccadilloes private, he was also in the habit of keeping a pair of doll's panties in his pocket. Whatever bar he was in, if he was feeling playful, he would put them on his fingers and 'dance' across the counter of the bar.

Whenever he went out with friends he would surreptitiously jot down phrases from their conversations on scraps of paper. Once back home, he would then use his friend's words as the basis of some of the dialogue for his novels.

A few years after *Ulysses* was published, he had an affair with a young woman whilst at a symposium in Zurich. He apparently met her at a unisex toilet and fell for her, he told a friend, 'at the very moment she pulled the chain'.

Joyce was remarkably candid about how he dealt with writer's block: he was a masturbator of a truly Olympian standard. There is a wonderful story about an attractive American lady who came up to him in the street and asked to shake the hand that wrote *Ulysses*. Apparently Joyce paused, closed his eyes, thought about it for a moment and then said 'I'd rather you didn't. It's done a few other things as well.'